Laugh out Loud: A User's Guide to Workplace Humor

Barbara Plester • Kerr Inkson

Laugh out Loud: A User's Guide to Workplace Humor

palgrave
macmillan

Barbara Plester
Management & International Business
University of Auckland Business School
Auckland, New Zealand

Kerr Inkson
University of Auckland Business School
Auckland, New Zealand

ISBN 978-981-13-0282-4   ISBN 978-981-13-0283-1   (eBook)
https://doi.org/10.1007/978-981-13-0283-1

Library of Congress Control Number: 2018951788

Cover illustration: © ColorBlind Images / Getty Images
Cover Design by Fatima Jamadar

This Palgrave Macmillan imprint is published by the registered company Springer Nature Singapore Pte Ltd.
The registered company address is: 152 Beach Road, #21-01/04 Gateway East, Singapore 189721, Singapore

ACKNOWLEDGMENTS

FROM BARBARA

To my wonderful co-author, Kerr—thank you for all your good humor, insights and most of all your talent for writing. I have relished the chance to learn from you, work with you and bounce ideas back and forth, usually accompanied by laughter. It has been fun working together and that's the point when writing a book like this!

I'd like to massively thank my wonderful, slightly crazy family, which keeps growing as new people join. All my love and thanks Paul, Riki and Jessie, Maxine, Andrew, Charlie and Archer, Bjorn and Cinnamon. My most heartfelt thanks to you all; I relish your love, life and laughter every day. Thanks also to Panda, Bowie, Dudley and Fergus—canine input is always welcome and 'walkies' are good for us all!

Mum (Irene) and Dad (Bryan) and my five brothers and sisters (Fil, Mark, Jax, Bad Al, and Kathryn) and their partners (Jody, Julie, Dave, and James), plus all your kids—too many to list. You are all a bit nutty, and I'm glad you are. Humor and fun always turn up when you all arrive. Keep laughing.

FROM KERR

My biggest thanks go to my co-author Barbara. I have found coauthoring this book a very pleasant and sociable task due to her years of patient research, encyclopedic knowledge of workplace humor, warm invitation to me to work with her, hard work and good humor in the process and her constant concern for the rank-and-file staff in the organizations we write about.

In the writing of 'practical' research-based books, various collaborators have given me the self-confidence to coauthor such books by allowing me to work on their material and providing great support and encouragement. That is true of Barbara, but also, of Nick Marsh, Gill Ellis, David Irving, Michael Arthur, David C Thomas, Yvonne McNulty and the late Brian Henshall.

I also want to thank my daughter Eileen in London and a couple of anonymous friends for allowing me to access a few of the true stories in this book. Thanks also to my wife Nan: while I buried myself in my study, writing, Nan as usual worked around her multiple voluntary activities to double up on housekeeping, and kept me going with encouragement and coffee.

From Both of Us

Enormous thanks go to all of our wonderful participants. Thank you for sharing your stories and humor and allowing us such honest access to your worlds. We could not have written this without you all.

We would like to thank Professor Arnie Cann for his encouragement to use, in Chap. 3, the Humor Culture Questionnaire, which he and his colleagues devised.

To our Palgrave Macmillan publication team: Vishal and Anu, thank you for your ongoing support, guidance and advice. Also to the production team (Jasper, Maha and team).

Finally, thank you to our fantastic colleagues at the University of Auckland Business School. You are always ready to drop in for a chat and a laugh—especially when we're looking at cat memes! Thank for you collegiality and laughter. At the University of Auckland and at other universities and organizations, our working lives have long been enriched by the quick-witted joking, banter, laughter and sheer good humor of countless colleagues. These are gifts for us to cherish, and to do what we can to pass on to others.

CONTENTS

About the Authors

Barbara Plester has needed to hone her own sense of humor to cope with her noisy, zany family, friends and pets. Born and bred in New Zealand (a 'kiwi'), she has researched humor and fun for the last 14 years. Such a research focus has elicited disbelief and ridicule but also intense interest at times. Based at the University of Auckland Business School for the past 11 years, Barbara has published academic papers in both humor and management journals, book chapters in edited volumes and a complete book of her humor research in 2016—*The Complexity of Workplace Humour,* Springer. She uses her humor research experiences in her teaching, highlighting the implications for workplace issues and organizational behavior. She has received two awards for excellence in teaching and was awarded 'Senior Fellowship' of the UK-based Higher Education Academy (SFHEA) in 2018. Chairing the Equity Committee for her faculty, Barbara has a keen interest in promoting tolerance and equity for all groups of people. Retaining her own sense of humor and fun at work and home, she tries hard to constantly maintain her mantra of 'laugh out loud!'

Kerr Inkson is a Scottish academic who emigrated to New Zealand when he was young. His field is organizational behavior, including research on work motivation and careers. In a 55-year career, he has served seven universities, five of them in New Zealand, including 25 years at the University of Auckland, where he is now an emeritus professor. Recently he has focused on book writing, always with coauthors who know more about the topic than he does, the most recent of his 20 books being *Managing Expatriates*, with Yvonne McNulty, 2013; *Understanding Careers*, with Nicky Dries and John Arnold, 2015; and *Cultural Intelligence* (3rd edition), with David C Thomas, 2017. Kerr's retirement hobbies are amateur dramatics, writing (including plays) and golf. His favorite radio and TV humor tends to British anarchic (*The Goon Show, Monty Python, Fawlty Towers*), improvisational (*Whose Line is It Anyway?, Qi*) and American-satirical (Stephen Colbert, John Oliver). He dislikes stand-up comedy, except for that of his compatriot, the incomparable Billy Connolly.

CHAPTER 1

Introducing Workplace Humor

Here's a typical example of workplace humor. What do you make of it?

Being Flexible
Ted and Mandy, engineers at XYZ Hydraulics, are working on different parts of the same design project. Ted approaches Mandy at her workplace.

Ted: 'We need to get together and compare where we're at.'
Mandy: 'We do.'
Ted: 'But when? I've got a lot on next week. But what about you? Are you flexible?'
Mandy: 'Flexible? Well, when I was a kid I could do the splits, but I don't know about now!'

Ted and Mandy laugh. Another worker, Josie, has overheard the last remark.

Josie (*to Mandy, smiling*):   'Why on earth are you telling him that?'
Ted (*tapping his nose*):   'Wouldn't you like to know? There's a lot about us you don't know!'

(Ted moves closer to Mandy and smiles at her. Ted and Mandy both laugh. Josie looks puzzled).

© The Author(s) 2019
B. Plester, K. Inkson, *Laugh out Loud: A User's Guide to Workplace Humor*, https://doi.org/10.1007/978-981-13-0283-1_1

Mandy's deliberate misunderstanding of the word 'flexible' was clever, and most likely you can see some humor, but not as much as Ted and Mandy saw. A key feature of any humor is *identification*. To find something funny, we need generally to identify with it, to have an underlying sympathy with the viewpoint of the humorist(s).

With workplace humor, this sympathy is often conveyed by the common phrase *you had to be there,* which suggests that the humor comes out of directly observing events rather than having them reported to you by a third party (in this case, the authors of this book). Also, you might appreciate the humor if you had some identification, understanding and/or sympathy with the people involved and the situation, for example knowing and feeling empathy for Ted and/or Mandy and their relationship.

In other words, workplace humor is highly *contextual,* and much of it can only be understood and felt by those with a good appreciation of the background situation, particularly past events and interpersonal relationships. For that reason, do not expect the many anecdotes in this book to be side-splittingly funny *you had to be there,* you had to know the people: you weren't, and you didn't!

Whether or not the Ted-Mandy-Josie interaction was funny, was it good or bad? Did it help those involved? They seemed to be enjoying themselves. Were some of them laughing just because others were? And what about getting their jobs done? What about the XYZ Hydraulics organization that was paying them? Wasn't the humor distracting them from their work, slowing them down, reducing productivity?

If there had been a manager there, would s/he have liked the exchange or found it silly and unproductive? Quite likely the manager would scarcely have noticed it, or would have thought, 'That's fine, people joke around a lot at work, it makes them feel good, it does no harm. It was the starting point for what may be a productive meeting between Ted and Mandy, it showed a good positive work relationship between the three of them and it took almost no time at all'.

On the other hand, humor is not always as straightforward as we may think. Sometimes the meaning of humor is a little more mysterious, even sinister. Why did Josie initially seem surprised by Mandy's joke about 'the splits'? And what do we make of Ted's vague remark that 'there's a lot about us you don't know?' Is he simply saying that he and Mandy are a good team, is he hinting at a closer relationship or trying to develop one? Is it ok for him to move closer to Mandy to dramatize the relationship he seems to be hinting at? Alternatively, is he simply putting Josie in her place, by implying that she is an 'outsider' to the Ted-and-Mandy 'in-group'?

Humor can go wrong. Consider another scenario in the Ted-Mandy-Josie story:

A Joke That Fell Flat

Ted:	'We need to get together and compare where we're at.'
Mandy:	'We do.'
Ted:	'But when? I've got a lot on next week. But what about you? Are you flexible?'
Mandy:	'Flexible? Well, when I was a kid I could do the splits, but I don't know about now!'
Ted *(laughing)*:	'The splits, eh? That's a sight I'd like to see! I'd love to see your split!'

He laughs loudly. Mandy joins in, uneasily. Josie has overheard Ted's last remark. She comes over.

Josie *(to Mandy)*:	'Are you all right?'
Mandy *(uncertain)*:	'I ... um .... Yes, I'm ok.'
Josie *(to Ted)*:	'That didn't sound very nice.'
Ted *(angry)*:	*'Back off! It was only a joke!'*

What is 'only a joke' to one person can be offensive, insulting or threatening to another. Ted's remark, 'the splits, eh? That's a sight I'd like to see! I'd love to see your split!' may have been a piece of innocent banter. But it could alternatively be viewed as a sexual innuendo or an expression of Ted's inner aggressiveness, or it might even actually have been one of those. What seems like an innocent joke may not be innocent to everyone. This second scenario resulted in Mandy being uneasy, Josie suspicious and Ted angry—none of them emotions conducive to harmonious or productive working relationships.

WORKPLACE HUMOR: THE GOOD AND THE BAD

Humor is nowadays a universal part of our working lives. It occurs in all countries and all cultures. It occurs in all settings: in relationships, in family life, in leisure pursuits. We even use humor introspectively, joking to ourselves when we are alone. So it isn't surprising that in the nearly 50% of our waking hours when we are working for our living, humor is typically to the fore, part and parcel of our working relationships with others.

Workplaces nowadays tend to be fairly functional. They need to be effective. They need to be efficient. This is achieved by the textbook combinations of people, money, resources, strategies, competitive advantage, workforce commitment, skills and so on. But *humor*? Humor, surely, can only be a distraction. What is workplace humor *for*? What can it do that makes the organization better at what it does?

Workplace humor is usually, though not always, good for us. We need it! Consider what happens when it is denied us. Both authors of this book have experience in humor repression:

Banishing Humor

Barbara: I once had a job where the boss forbade laughing at work. He said it was distracting and interfered with productivity. Otherwise the job was stimulating, in nice conditions and well paid. But that wasn't enough. Being in a no-laughter zone was too much for me, I had humor deprivation, and I left after three months. Others too left in droves, for the same reason. In contrast, my other jobs—sanding doors in a factory and packing groceries in a supermarket—were more mundane and poorly paid. But I liked them much better because I could use fun and laughter to make the hours go by.

Kerr: Many years ago—about 55, I think—I worked in a pea cannery in Scotland —a summer job. I was the 'can-loft' boy, darting around in the summer heat in an attic store of cardboard boxes of empty cans, fetching, unfolding the boxes and setting them in front of the can-girls, who would place the cans on runners to run down into the factory. At peak season, we were working 14 hours a day. It was soul destroying and tedious. We had two ways of coping—singing and laughing. The humor helped the time to pass. But eventually Bob, our alcoholic supervisor, actually fired me for joking! There was nothing especially offensive about my banter, and none of it was directed at him—at least not when he was in earshot. He just couldn't stand us having a good time.

Barbara and Kerr: In contrast to those stories, our many combined years of work as university academics have frequently been joyful times, enriched by the good humor and the sheer funniness of some of those around us. We have worked hard, done well and generally been in a good mood created partly by the positive, clever use of humor by so many of our colleagues. We have laughed at, and with, others, and been laughed at by them, but nearly always in a gentle, good-humored way that seldom caused offense. Without humor, our university careers might have been worthy but would have been very, very dull and might well have been less productive.

And so, our experiences have convinced us that humor in organizations is a gift, a practice that, done the right way, makes work a pleasure and probably enhances performance. Humor provides a lighter side to the serious business of work. It gets us laughing—and therefore feeling good—even if we are not personally involved in the joke. It lightens the load, makes the hours pass more quickly and turns work relationships into friendships through the sharing of laughter. Good-natured workplace banter, shared in-jokes, gentle laughter at our own minor foibles and those of our colleagues, shared jokes about our organization's bosses or bureaucracy or advertising or customers: these are part and parcel of most working lives. Laughter is inherently pleasurable. It makes us feel good, not only about ourselves but also about the colleagues we are sharing it with. Thus, most of the time, humor appears to be a positive experience for us and a productive one for our organizations. Working relationships prosper; morale rises; productivity benefits; everyone wins.

At the same time, humor can go badly wrong, even in the workplace, as it did in the second Ted-Mandy-Josie scenario. If staff overindulge in joking, working time can vanish and productivity may fall. One person's humor can be deeply offensive or hurtful or just plain boring to another, damaging the very relationships it is intended to foster and leading to ill-feeling and mistrust. And, in these 'politically correct' times, humor that may have seemed acceptable a decade or two ago may no longer be so.

Funny Ha-ha, Funny Peculiar or Unfunny Disgusting?

Gregor and his girlfriend Margot (not their real names), were transient immigrants with work experience on ski fields. They found work with the same ski company but on different fields. On Margot's field, the ski company, attempting to promote morale, introduced a 'woo week' event. An event poster encouraged staff to 'Let those romantic and creative juices flow, to show your affections and/or appreciation for your woo-ee. Whether you're single, married, de facto or other, woo week is fun for everyone. You are assigned at random one person to woo in secret from 23rd to –29th July'. Employees were thus encouraged to boost this person's morale with notes and gifts.

At first, Margot found Post-it notes from her male woo-er telling her 'I love watching you work'. But one day, she returned to her work space to find a handwritten note on pink paper that said: 'Margot, this is all for you baby xxx'. Beside it sat a condom which had been left to look as if it had been used. It was filled with mayonnaise. Other workers knew all about the joke even before it was played. Margot felt horrified and humiliated. She complained to management, who, following what they called 'stringent anti-harassment and anti-bullying policy' gave the man a formal warning.

Margot asked for a transfer to her boyfriend's ski field, where she would feel safer. This was denied by the company. Margot and Gregor resigned but found getting alternative work difficult.

While we can't know for sure, we are guessing that the man responsible for this 'joke', and perhaps some of his friends with whom he shared it, would have thought the 'gift' hilarious. What do you think? That the man involved was making an innocent joke, and that prissy Margot couldn't take the joke, and overreacted? That the joke was in bad taste, and that the man should have known better, but that it was scarcely a disciplinary offense? Or that the joke was disgusting and offensive sexual harassment, that any self-respecting woman would have acted as Margot did, and that the man should have been fired, or at least removed from working anywhere near Margot? Perhaps by the end of this book you will have a better basis for answering this question, and a clearer understanding of why the man acted as he did, and why Margot responded as she did.

At all events, the story shows us that humor is often contentious and can lead to major problems of discipline, morale, teamwork and even legality in organizations. Humor, in short, is a topic that sometimes should be taken very, very seriously!

WHY YOU NEED TO READ THIS BOOK

Because of humor's potential to create both good and harm in the workplace, it is increasingly clear that it needs to be *managed,* both by organizational humorists and by every manager of every organizational unit or department where it is used—and that means virtually every manager in the world! In addition, as we show particularly in Chap. 10, everyone has a role in getting humor 'right' in organizations—not just humorists and managers, but those it is directed toward, victims such as Margot in the case above, HR people and others with responsibility for making and applying policies and procedures affecting workplace humor, and even observers—those who witness humor without being part of it. Hence this book.

When we began to prepare a proposal to send to Palgrave Macmillan as prospective publishers of this book, and we investigated both the potential market for a practical book on the management of workplace humor, and the potential competition—other books on the same topic—we received a huge surprise. *We could not—and still cannot—find any other book like this on the market, anywhere!*

Instead, what we found was this. First, there is a huge body of *academic* research and theory on humor, including workplace humor. Researchers such as Barbara have literally sat at the back of organizational rooms for years, observing and analyzing the humor that went on in them. Others have done systematic quantitative studies of humor, measuring it and dissecting it. Theories and analyses of humor exist in literary studies, anthropology, sociology, psychology, linguistics and many other fields. This provides a strong basis for understanding how humor works, both in workplaces and in other settings, and we will make good use of such knowledge in this book.

On the other hand, these books appear to be largely written *by* academics *for* academics, using abstract theory and language largely inaccessible to the average user of humor. Barbara is the author of one such book, *The Complexity of Workplace Humor* (Springer, 2016). That book is based on her 14 years of research in the area—much of this time spent sitting in on sundry workplaces as a 'fly-on-the-wall', observing and taking notes on all the humor around her, and interviewing the staff involved as to what they found funny and why. That book is (in the view of the other author, Kerr) as fine a compendium as you will find, of academic understanding of how workplace humor works, and an excellent resource for scholars and students of humor.

However, even this fine book contains little information to guide the activities of the actual *producers and consumers* of workplace humor—organization members—and it is these people that our book is for. They come in several categories:

- the organizational *humorists* or *initiators* of humor, some of whom initiate humor to such an extent that they become known as organizational *jokers*;
- the *targets* at whom humor is directed, who sometimes, if the humor is offensive or humiliating, become *victims*;
- the rank-and-file *observers* of humor, who see, hear and respond to humor, and who sometimes, if the humor is entertaining, become an *audience*;
- the people we call *gatekeepers*, who try to control the humor so that it doesn't cause offense or get out of hand: some of them are *formal gatekeepers*, often HR people; others are rank-and-file employees, *informal gatekeepers* who like to keep the organization feeling 'right'; and
- the *managers* who have to manage workplace humor—including contentious incidents such as the ski field one described above—so that it is a positive rather than a negative force in the workplace.

If you are in one or more of these categories, we believe, you probably need a more practical book than the ones the academics offer. In the present book, we therefore attempt to distill the research-based wisdom of Barbara's book into a simpler story that not only helps you to understand workplace humor better but also gives you some practical pointers to managing it.

A second type of book available on the market—though here we were able to locate only a few—is those about workplace humor written by managers and management consultants with extensive workplace experience. These books, however, tend (a) to cover humor only as a subset of a broader 'human relations' approach to workplace management; (b) lack any understanding of the considerable amount that is known about humor through academic research; and (c) take a relentlessly positive ('cheerleader') approach to workplace humor and totally fail to recognize its 'dark side'.

We are therefore unable to recommend any book we have seen, neither the academic nor the practitioner type, as either alternative or support reading to this book. As far as we are concerned, THIS BOOK IS IT! If you want to learn, in layman's terms, the best and latest research-based information about how workplace humor works and how you can best practice it or manage it, this is where you come. Congratulations on the wisdom of your choice!

Who This Book Is for

Humorists/Jokers

A Natural Comedian
Kerr: When I was a patrol leader in the Boy Scouts, Jacob was in my patrol. Jacob was the smallest, youngest boy in the troop, 12 years old, scrawny, unathletic, with an odd, rubbery, flushed face. Not the kind of person you would expect to have much power in an outfit that fancied itself as rather macho.

But Jacob had a gift. Not only was he highly intelligent, he was one of the *funniest* people I have ever met. It was low-key humor, slightly self-deprecating. He had an eye for everything slightly out of the ordinary that was going on around him, and his deadpan quips and his mimicking of those in authority would reduce all around him to helpless laughter. He could make you laugh by merely raising an eyebrow. When we went on our summer scout camp, the other scouts clustered around him: everyone would have a good time when Jacob was in the group. At night, we were glad to have him in our cabin. His constant jokes and tomfoolery entranced us, and we fell asleep with smiles on our faces.

> But one night he didn't come back to our cabin. The next day we found out he had spent the night in a spare bunk in another patrol's cabin. When we asked him why, he just said, 'They paid me—I'm in demand, you see'. And he let a big smile spread across his face.
>
> He knew what was happening. At 12, he was a professional comic.

Don't think you can necessarily do what Jacob did—few people can. He had a special gift for humor, and you may not. Psychological research tells us that by the time most people join the workforce, their basic level of humorousness has already been determined mostly by their childhood experiences and learning. Your humor, and your responses to others' humor, have therefore been developed from your unique abilities and personal characteristics: we can't change that and wouldn't try.

Do you see yourself as being like Jacob, a naturally humorous person? Or, with less natural talent than he had, have you developed something of an ability to make others laugh? Do you find others expect you to joke, and seem to enjoy it when you do? Or perhaps you are not a humorous person but work in a place where there is an expectation that most people will have a sense of humor, and make the odd joke? Our task in this book is to help both the natural jokers and the occasional ones to understand what is actually going on behind their humor, and to show all of you its potential and its risks.

What we can do is make you more aware of how humor—including your humor—works, what your use of it may say about you and how it may affect others. We can show you that some of your humor may be positive and life enhancing for others, but that other humor, or even the same humor, may, unbeknown to you, offend and damage other people, your relationships and the organizations you work for, in ways and to an extent that you may not appreciate.

We can show you how to use humor in a more sensitive and productive way, the bonus being that you may become even funnier. Humor is a precious gift, potentially a beautiful light in many people's lives. But it has to be properly nurtured and used.

Targets/Victims

Much workplace humor is directed to, at, or against particular individuals. This can range from friendly banter to aggressive hostility disguised as humor. For example, imagine a super-punctual individual who always turns up early for meetings. The person she is visiting may respond with, 'Joan, you're late! You're only five minutes early!' (friendly banter) or with 'Early again, Joan? Greasing up the boss, eh, Ms. Goody Two-Shoes?' (aggressive ridicule). The latter type of remark, although rarer, is hard to deal with. Targets of this type of humor are sometimes referred to as 'victims'. How should they respond?

Observers/Audience

Observers of workplace humor nether initiate humor, nor are they targets of it. They see and hear workplace humor, may or may not be amused by it, and may or may not become involved, changing from the role of observer to that of humorist or target. If this is you, you too have a role to play in the evolution of humor in the organizations you work for. Observers respond to humor, for example with laughter or disgust, and these responses shape humor.

So you, as an observer of humor, can influence how workplace humor develops, or doesn't develop. Humor often amuses, but it can also offend, insult or humiliate. How do you react when you are offended by a joke? Laugh (because everyone else is), deliberately avoid laughing, frown, tell the joker you feel offended or complain to higher authority? Responses to present humor can change future humor.

Gatekeepers: Informal

Another, perhaps smaller, group are those who deliberately attempt to influence workplace humor, generally in the direction of seeking to curtail humor that they find offensive and/or that they think is inappropriate. We call them gatekeepers because they seek to influence what happens within the organization's 'gates'. Because the humorists or jokers initiating humor are often men, who have greater tolerance for sexist, sexual and racist humor than women, informal gatekeepers are very often female. Typically they will intervene by asking the humorists, in the words of one we observed, to 'keep the party clean, boys'. As we will see, much depends on their understanding of the humor culture of the organization and the respect in which they are held by others.

Gatekeepers: Formal

These are members of the organization who are formally expected to control organizational humor by designing and imposing organizational policies and procedures covering humor. Of course, few organizations have formal policies on humor, but many have more general policies which may be breached by the inappropriate use of humor. Examples are policies on offensive language and behavior, equal employment opportunity, rights of gays, lesbians, women and people with disabilities, ageism and sexual harassment and other forms of bullying. Crude humor can easily breach the principles of such guidelines, and many organizations seek to protect their employees, and expect centrally located staff, particularly in the HR function, to ensure compliance and investigate breaches.

Such staff may be disparagingly referred to by miscreants as 'politically correct' and/or 'the humor police'. In the same way that the actual police are nowadays encouraged to focus on crime prevention as well as on crime detection and punishment, so too can organizational gatekeepers learn about fostering the kind of humor environment and culture which makes breaches of policy rare. They too may be able to read, reflect and learn from this book.

Managers

Finally, and perhaps most importantly, this book is for *managers*: those who have to manage workplaces where humor is part of the working day, and that's just about every workplace that there is on the planet. As we have shown, workplace humor is inevitable, and potentially morale boosting. It is an integral part of the organization's or work group's culture, and a means of 'setting the tone' on which organization or group performance is based. But it has its downside. It can get out of hand, distract, offend, or oppress individual workers and destroy social cohesion and organizational performance. The story above, of Margot, the ski instructor shocked by a vulgar, thoughtless joke, is a case in point.

This means that all managers must be managers of humor. They need not necessarily be humorists themselves: some managers talented at humor can use humor very effectively in their jobs, but in most cases a managerial role puts constraints on humor (see Chap. 7).

If you are a manager, how can you use humor productively and manage the humor of others so as to protect the vulnerable, make staff feel good, build team cohesion, celebrate success and avoid offense or conflict? With the right knowledge and tools, you can do all these things: you just need to be able to *see and understand* what is going on behind the comedy in your workplace, observe when it is having positive or negative effects and know whether, when and how to intervene. Again, read, reflect and learn from this book.

WHAT THIS BOOK CAN'T DO

We do, however, wish to tell you what we cannot do in this book. As outlined above, we cannot make you funny—the organizational 'joker'. We cannot teach you jokes that never fail to entertain. While we can help you understand how funny people work their magic, they have become the way they are through their personality, identity and their lifetime of unique personal experiences and experiments, which you cannot replicate.

WHAT THIS BOOK CAN DO

Our task in this book then, is to present to you the best and most up-to-date knowledge we can, based on the best theory and research we know, of how humor works, particularly in the workplace, and what effects it has. We also want to help you to use humor if you are a joker, respond to it if you are a target or observer, manage it if you are a manager and regulate it if you are a policymaker.

To achieve these objectives, we draw your attention to four characteristics you will find in every chapter:

1. *A sound knowledge base.* We know a lot about workplace humor. Barbara is a world authority on it, who has spent 15 years studying it, observing it patiently for many days as a 'fly-on-the-wall' in many organizations and later interviewing those involved. She also knows the humor research of other researchers from all over the world and the key theories of humor. Kerr is less of a specialist but has been fascinated by how organizations work and has been a professor of Organizational Behavior for many years and has written many books. And between us, we have had perhaps 80 years of being employees and managers. So we have lots of relevant experience and knowledge to bring to bear.

So much is known about humor through research that we absolutely have to use it as the knowledge base of the book. We'd be wasting your time if we didn't. But we'll try to make it as simple and practical as possible. However, should you want to access our sources, or visit some of the websites we refer to, or delve further into the subject and gain deeper insights, you will find a comprehensive set of 'references, notes and further reading' at the end of the book.

2. *Stories.* People love concrete, real-life stories to illustrate practical principles. So this book is illustrated by 'vignettes'—little stories, such as the Ted-and-Mandy story, exemplifying workplace humor. These are taken mainly from our research and day-to-day experience, from others' experience, from the Net, from wherever we could find them, sometimes slightly disguised to protect identification. Many of them are from the various organizations whose humor Barbara has studied in her research, and we also have some stories from the television industry via an informant in a company called Victory TV and a few others from miscellaneous sources. We weave the stories into the text and explain each one so that you can not only enjoy it but also understand the point it illustrates.

3. *Everyday language.* We are academics, and we academics tend to use longer and less understandable words than we need to. Without unnecessarily 'dumbing down' our content, we have tried to keep the academic jargon to a minimum and to explain any unusual terms we use.

4. *'Takeaways'.* An MBA student once said to us, 'I want you to tell me stuff today that I can take away and use in practice in my organization tomorrow'. Nowadays this is called a 'takeaway'. While not all learning can be applied quite as immediately as this student wanted, and while every reader will have his or her unique situation to deal with, we do understand where the student was coming from. Accordingly, each of Chaps. 2, 3, 4, 5, 6, 7, 8 and 9 will have a brief 'takeaway' section of practical applications at its conclusion. Because our major focus on the *management* of humor, these will mainly be for that group. Chapter 10 includes takeaways for all our readerships: initiators, jokers, targets, observers, gatekeepers and managers.

CAVEAT

Before you get into this book, we have a warning to issue.

In everyday organizational life, in both humorous and non-humorous situations, some people use language that others may find offensive. In our observation of humorous interactions at work, we noted frequent use of two words, sometimes referred to elsewhere as 'the f-word' and 'the s-word', both 'four-letter words'. The f-word is often used not only in its original meaning of sexual intercourse but (sometimes with the suffix'-ing' added) also as an expression of frustration or anger, a substitute for the word 'very', or for 'do something nasty to you' and so on. Likewise, the s-word is frequently used to refer to things such as bureaucracy, procedures, sentiments the speaker doesn't agree with and so on.

In presenting the many stories in this book to illustrate various aspects of workplace humor, we wish to be authentic: to present events exactly as they happened. Although we ourselves do not normally use the f-word or the s-word in our own talk, and will not often write them into our own text, we will therefore, in our illustrative stories, use our characters' actual language, including these terms, as accurately as we can remember it. Moreover, we will not be writing 'sh*t' or 'f-ck', we will be writing 'shit' and 'fuck'. This enables us to remain true to both the actual words spoken by our characters and the spirit in which they used them. If these words have offended you, we apologize, and we suggest you stop reading this book now!

THE REST OF THIS BOOK

What can you expect in the remaining chapters of this book? While we have tried to set them out in a logical order, we understand that not everyone is 'linear' in the way they approach books, so we encourage you, if you wish, to move around the book, looking for the ideas that most interest you. You may even want to flick through some of the boxed humor stories to get an idea of some of the actual humor we have observed in workplaces, before proceeding to the theory and 'how-to-do-it' bits.

To assist you, here's a kind of chapter-by-chapter map:

Chapter 2, 'How humor works' is not especially related to workplaces. Instead it explains the importance of context to humor—what we call the 'you had to be there' phenomenon. It outlines the main academic theories that are now understood to underlie most humor, including workplace humor—showing how it is mostly based on incongruity, superiority or aggression, tension release and sociability.

In Chap. 3, 'Humor cultures', we look at humor as an organizational norm. Comparing a 'low-humor' organization with a 'moderate-humor' and a 'high-humor' one, we show how each organization has its own humor norms and boundaries and how it develops and maintains them. We also provide a validated questionnaire that you and your colleagues can complete to measure the humor culture in your organization.

In Chap. 4, 'Doing humor', we detail the main forms that workplace humor can take. We cover banter in detail because it is probably the most common form of workplace humor. We deal with 'canned jokes', pranks and horseplay. In each case, we indicate some of the benefits and dangers.

In Chap. 5, 'Ritual humor', we note that humor often becomes ritual, being demonstrated or enhanced in specific events such as 'managed fun' organized by the organization's bosses, presentations, celebrations, ceremonies and the like. Ritual can also emerge spontaneously from different groups' actions. Again, we describe some typical ritual events and note how their humor may help or hinder.

Chapter 6, 'Technological humor', recognizes the fact that increasingly workplace humor involves the use of new information technology and is presented in images and text rather than face-to-face. We deal with emoji and emoticons, memes, websites and other office artefacts, and with the use of email for the distribution of humor. Again, we focus on pros and cons.

Chapter 7, 'Joker's wild', deals with those larger-than-life figures who are in nearly every workplace and are known as the 'joker'. Who are they, and how, and why, do they do what they do? We note that most jokers are men rather than women and consider the different humor styles of these two genders. We observe that not all jokers are good at the job and examine what some of the pitfalls are in being, or seeking to be, a workplace joker.

Chapter 8 is called 'The bright side of humor'. We note that much humor is derived from positive motives and intentions from those who initiate it and document observable positive effects on morale, teamwork and stress reduction. We also discuss the positive health effects of laughter, the 'Pollyanna' effect and overly optimistic humor. We consider possible effects on productivity and performance.

Chapter 9 on 'The dark side of humor' is a contrast. Here we seek to puncture the sometimes-popular view that humor is always a good thing, by showing the downside: humor as a deliberate or inadvertent means of offense and humiliation and aggression; humor in the service of domination, power and even violence or the reinforcement of prejudice; and negative humor as a tool of resistance by disaffected employees.

In Chap. 10, 'The Management of Humor', we consolidate the entire contents of Chaps. 2, 3, 4, 5, 6, 7, 8 and 9 into offering advice—further 'takeaways' if you like—to each of the various client groups mentioned earlier in this chapter: humorists /jokers, targets/victims, observers/audience, informal gatekeepers, formal gatekeepers, and managers. We try to give each of these groups ideas, derived from our analysis, about what they can actually *do* about workplace humor in their particular role.

That is the plan—on with the book!

CHAPTER 2

How Humor Works

Joke Work

Here are two jokes; the first is an excerpt from a popular television comedy, the second is an old Scottish joke:

Joke 1: What is a Sagittarius?

Penny: 'I'm a Sagittarius, which probably tells you way more than you need to know.'

Sheldon: 'Yes, it tells us that you participate in the mass cultural delusion that the sun's apparent position relative to arbitrarily defined constellations at the time of your birth somehow affects your personality.'

(Excerpt from the television comedy *The Big Bang Theory*)

Joke 2: Crocodile at large

Jock walks into a Glasgow bar. Walking with him is a crocodile, on a lead like a dog.

Jock addresses the barman. 'Do you serve Catholics?' he enquires.

© The Author(s) 2019
B. Plester, K. Inkson, *Laugh out Loud: A User's Guide to Workplace Humor*, https://doi.org/10.1007/978-981-13-0283-1_2

'Yes, of course we do', says the barman.
'In that case', says Jock, 'a whiskey for me and a Catholic for the crocodile'.
(This joke was current in Scotland, especially Glasgow, in the 1950s.)

Do you find these jokes funny? It's unlikely anybody finds them hilarious. Probably some readers found them mildly amusing, some didn't find them funny at all, some found them stupid and some found the second one distasteful. But whether you found them funny or not, they give us the opportunity to think about some of the key characteristics of humor. Those who find them funny will most likely have smiled, perhaps even laughed, thereby experiencing a moment or two of a warm, positive internal sensation: there are apparently humor centers in the frontal lobes of the brain. Humor thus has the potential to give *pleasure*.

Both jokes also indicate the 'incongruity' theory of humor. Much humor is based on ideas that are unusual and bizarre. In Joke 1, Penny thinks that informing Sheldon of her Zodiac sign tells him—as in everyday newspaper horoscopes—about her personality traits, and that Sheldon will understand this. However, his reply is incongruous because, perhaps due to his background in science and consequent disbelief in astrology, he suggests that her belief in such matters tells him something completely different about her. This is not the response she was expecting and as viewers we understand this and see the joke as Sheldon brings a different (incongruous) interpretation to the interaction. In Joke 2, the idea of a man taking a pet crocodile into a bar, and the play on words that turns the Catholic from a customer into a crocodile's meal are both unexpected and bizarre. In short, much, if not most, humor is based on the *incongruous*.

Humor thus transports us, forcefully and intriguingly, out of our everyday world into another one that doesn't quite play by the normal rules. Humor breaks normal conventions governing how we should think, reason and talk. Humor is therefore at least mildly *anarchic*.

Both jokes also illustrate the 'superiority' theory of humor: Sheldon's derision of astrology as a 'mass cultural delusion' suggests he feels superior to Penny as he mocks her beliefs; women seeing or hearing this joke might be irritated by its echoes of societal stereotypes of 'dumb' women and smart 'rocket scientist' men. In Joke 2, Catholics as food for crocodiles are treated as inferior. As we will see, we often use humor as psychological prop—a weapon against others, or a crutch for our own sense of worth-whileness and indeed superiority in our social circle. Humor is often *therapeutic* and often *social*.

If you are a fan of *The Big Bang Theory*, you will recognize the characters and the style of Sheldon's putting-down commentary with affection and enjoyment. You will be able to hear, in your mind, his cutting monotone and the world-weary acceptance of Penny as she receives yet another Sheldon lecture about societal behaviors. You may think about, perhaps even anticipate, what the other *Big Bang* characters—Leonard, Howard, Raj, Bernadette and Amy—would contribute to the conversation. However, if you have never watched this, how will you know or understand these characters? While many people may get an idea of what the joke means, only *Big Bang Theory* fans will understand the background, the characters, the interpersonal dynamics. And the joke, if relayed secondhand, will lose much of its humor. You had to be there. You had to be able to picture it. You had to understand the people. The more you know about the background, the funnier you are likely to find the joke. As already stated in Chap. 1, humor is *contextualized*.

Some readers (perhaps Catholics) may have found the crocodile joke not only unfunny but positively distasteful. (Sorry if we upset you, but we have a point to make.) The idea of a crocodile eating a human being, these people might say, is never funny. And isn't the joke a straightforward example of religious prejudice and hostility against a particular group, even a veiled threat? If it was deliberately told to a Catholic in an aggressive or lip-licking manner, the listener might feel vaguely threatened. Humor can be, and frequently is, *offensive*.

Humor that seems funny to one person may be offensive to another. Humor is in the eye of the beholder, or the ear of the listener. Humor is ambiguous, and subject to multiple interpretations. One person's hilarious joke is another person's humiliating insult. Humor is therefore *controversial*.

So, humor is potentially pleasurable, anarchic, therapeutic, social, contextualized, offensive and controversial. And, as we stated in Chap. 1, it is also ubiquitous, in workplaces as much as anywhere else. So, with all these possible benefits, drawbacks and uncertainties around humor, what on earth can a manager do with it?

Contextualizing Humor: 'You Had to Be there!'

Let's start off with contextualization. The most important thing to understand about workplace humor is what we called in Chap. 1 the 'you-had-to-be-there' phenomenon. And you have to be there not just in the sense of being physically present but also in the sense of understanding the context.

Have you ever been in a situation where you were a newcomer or stranger, and someone else made an apparently innocuous remark which caused the others present to laugh and laugh, whereas you couldn't see anything funny and couldn't understand what was going on? That is very common, because so much humor is based on a shared understanding (between joker and audience) of the situation.

Similarly, to fully appreciate the 'crocodile' joke above, you need to understand that in the mid- twentieth century when the joke was first coined, Glasgow was well known as being a hotbed of strife between Scottish Protestants and Irish Catholics. That rivalry provided a social *context* for the joke: so, to be really amused, you needed to hear the joke in Glasgow in, say, 1950. And perhaps you needed to be a Protestant rather than a Catholic. Context includes attitudes and relationships as well as physical location.

Workplace humor, because it takes place in specific situations involving people who typically work together for most of their waking hours and face common and ongoing organizational issues, is perhaps the most context specific of all. Relevant factors include the organization's culture; the background, history, situation and relationships of those involved; and their attitudes, for example how they feel about aggressiveness or sexual content or racial stereotypes expressed in a joke.

Thus, a joke or prank that would have everyone screaming with laughter in the accounts department of organization A might be greeted with incomprehension, distaste and/or hostility in organization B, or in another department of organization A, or even in the same department with different people present. In the background of each situation encountered within the organization—such as Ted-Josie-Mandy in Chap. 1—there is a history of company actions, of personal situations, interpersonal relationships, in-jokes and even 'things we don't talk about here'.

Why Is Everyone Laughing?
Your friend Madison works for Victory TV and has been invited to an expensive organizational function. Madison has invited you to accompany her. The event is the farewell party for Catherine, a long-

service employee who has been a wonderful mentor to Madison and a very effective and successful producer. She has made wonderful, best-selling programs, including the acclaimed, award-winning serial *Jaguar Bay* for Victory but has chosen to move on, to a professorship of television studies at a prestigious university.

At the function, her team has put together a leaving video, full of excerpts of people talking about Catherine and how much she will be missed. The video includes an interview with Gary, a senior Victory executive. But as you watch, it seems something has gone wrong. When Gary speaks to thank Catherine, he looks unenthusiastic, almost puzzled. In a totally deadpan voice, he says, 'Catherine who? I don't know who that is. I'm sorry. *Jaguar Bay*? No, that's my series. She didn't create it, I did. No, no you're mistaken—there wasn't any Catherine involved. It was my idea...Here's my award—this is the award I won for that series. *My* series. My *award-winning* series'.

This is terrible! Your friend's mentor is being insulted, at her own farewell party, by Victory's 'top brass'! Why is Gary whoever-he-is saying such things? And why have they been included in the video, and why is it being shown there? Do they want to humiliate Catherine? And then you notice something else odd. Despite Gary's dreadful claiming of Catherine's achievements for himself, and his seeming not even to know who she is, everyone else at the party is *laughing*! They love it. And Catherine is laughing along with them. *What on earth is going on? Why is everyone laughing?* You are utterly confused.

Later Madison explains to you. A major bugbear of television people at Victory (as in many TV production companies), is the tendency of the top executives to claim all the credit for successful programs they have in fact had very little to do with, leaving those who have done the real hard work, such as Catherine, Madison, and the other party guests, with no kudos at all. Gary is not like that, but he understands it; so his television speech is, to the party guests, a hilarious satire on the behavior of his own peers. It is funny to everyone involved because it touches a very raw nerve.

Once you understand that, it all makes sense. But to understand it, you not only had to be there, you had to be in on the group's feelings about 'who gets credit', and therefore in on the joke.

The 'you had to be there' injunction therefore involves much more than understanding whether the organization is a 'jokey' one or not. If you are a newcomer to such a company, you will have to tread especially carefully before letting fly with your favorite humor:

> **Saying the Wrong Thing**
> During Leon's first week in the open-plan office at his new job, an office assistant made a particularly silly mistake in the redirection of mail. After the assistant had apologized and left the room, one of the other employees explained to Leon that the assistant in question had made a number of similar mistakes, was on his last warning, and probably wouldn't last long in the company. 'I don't think he's very bright', explained the colleague.
>
> The remark put Leon in mind of a joke he had heard on the TV the previous night, a joke about a person with an intellectual disability working in an office. (For the sake of good taste, we won't repeat the joke here.) Leon, who fancied himself as a humorist, worked hard at telling the joke and delivered the punch line with panache. To his astonishment, this was followed not by laughter but by an embarrassed silence. Michelle at the next desk was staring at him and looked ready to cry. Then she abruptly rushed from the room. Another woman followed her, giving Leon an exasperated look as she went.
>
> 'I don't – what's wrong with her?' stammered Leon.
>
> His colleague shook his head. 'You weren't to know', he said, 'but she has a teenage daughter at home with an intellectual disability'.

All of us can probably remember those 'oh, shit!' moments when we have made such mistakes. Clearly, although using humor at work is often pleasurable and rewarding, it is also risky. Therefore, our first rule of workplace humor, for both humorists and managers, is **KNOW THE CONTEXT.** In particular, know the people you are joking to, or with. If Leon had known Michelle's personal situation he would not have made the joke he did. Knowing *context* and *observers* are key to the sensitivities needed by organizational humorists.

Despite our comments about humor being context specific, however, there are few situations where the right *kind* of humor cannot be used, provided it is used sensitively. Even funerals are lightened and humanized when a friend or relation recalls humorous events from the deceased person's life: the mourners titter as they recall these pleasurable moments of laughter, and even feel that by enjoying the jokes they are honoring the deceased. Humor can brighten up the darkest moments. But judging the fine line between the humor that satisfies and the humor that offends is, at best, tricky.

UNDERSTANDING HUMOR

The question often asked is 'What is humor?' A common answer is 'Does it matter? If it's funny, it's funny, there's no point in analyzing it. Humor is there to be enjoyed, not understood'. Most of us accept humor and laughter as a given, something to be experienced and enjoyed but not something to be analyzed.

The laughter phenomenon is intriguing, though. What is it, exactly, that makes us laugh out loud, or smile to ourselves, and to perceive what we experienced to be *funny?* And when we initiate humor, tell jokes, mock others, or enjoy the humor of others, what are we trying to achieve? What is the motivation?

It may be worth finding out. Humorists can gain insight from such an analysis, and perhaps improve their 'performance'. Managers who can tease out why certain things make us laugh will be in a better position to promote, control and manage humor in the workplace. From the pre-Christian eras, philosophers such as Socrates, Plato and Aristotle have theorized about the basis of humor. More recently, psychologists such as Sigmund Freud and psychological researchers have sought to identify the roots of humor in the human mind.

Here's an example:

Laughing at Colbert
In August 2017, while we were drafting this chapter, we watched, online, a clip of American talk show host Stephen Colbert delivering a monologue on the behavior of then White House communications chief Anthony Scaramucci (remember him? He didn't last long!).

While Colbert had an important point to make—about the poor communication skills of an important communications professional—the main effect was to reduce us—and the members of Colbert's studio audience—to uncontrollable, helpless laughter. This was done partly through the actual words and ideas that Colbert used but also through his dramatization of the events he was describing, particularly his impersonations of both Scaramucci and President Donald Trump. He used Scaramucci's reported obscene language and aggressive imagery to show the dramatic contrast with the expected suave presentation of a skilled media communicator. For example, Scaramucci had accused other White House personnel of being 'back-stabbers', and had described himself as a 'front-stabbing guy'. The punchline featured Colbert wielding an imaginary dagger in front of him and repeatedly stabbing forward with it while shouting 'Front-stab! Front-stab!' The result was very funny—but only, of course, to those who shared Colbert's political views.

Before we consider why many people found the Colbert skit funny, let's first note the contextualization. We can, to an extent, choose our contexts for humor—for example, choosing to watch Colbert's show in the first place. To find something funny, we also need generally to have an identification with the situation being portrayed, an understanding of some of the background factors (e.g. the political situations referred to, the controversial nature of the Trump presidency) and probably underlying sympathy with the viewpoint of the humorist. So when fans of Colbert and haters of Trump joined the studio audience or switched on their computers, they were contextualizing themselves in a place they knew would echo their views. Most likely they were people who laugh at Colbert's antics on a regular basis. When we watched Colbert and laughed, we not only had to be there, and we not only had to understand the context, we had to be who we were.

Supporters of Scaramucci and Trump, in contrast, would first of all know what to expect from Colbert and would not view the program. If they did see it, they might turn their TV or computer off or switch to another channel in disgust. What is funny is not a constant, but varies with the background and attitudes of the individuals who experience it. This works for workplace humor too—when a particular joker starts being funny, some employees may hurriedly move out of earshot or place their smartphone headphones in their ears: they literally can't stand it.

But why did many people find the Colbert skit funny?

Here are some possible answers:

- We—and the audience—laughed because of the ridiculousness, or *incongruity*, of the situation.
- We laughed because the presentation made us feel *superior* to Scaramucci and Trump.
- We laughed because it helped us to *relieve tension and stress*.
- We laughed because of the affirmation of a *relationship*, or fellow feeling, with Colbert and the others who were also laughing.

These explanations represent the four main *theories* of humor—explanations of what it is that makes certain stories, observations and events seem funny to observers, and what we get out of humor for ourselves. None of these theories is adequate, by itself, to explain all humor, but by combining them we can arrive at a reasonable explanation of how humor works.

THEORY 1: HUMOR THROUGH INCONGRUITY

'Incongruous' means inappropriate, out of place. If an idea is presented that is way outside the expectations that observers have, the resulting sense of absurdity frequently creates the sensation of funniness and the response of laughter. In the Colbert skit, for example, television viewers expect a high-profile communications director to be a skilled communicator, articulate and diplomatic. Instead he is portrayed as a coarse, clumsy buffoon.

However, incongruity by itself is not enough. If you remark that you saw a carrot growing out of a silicon chip, the image is incongruous but not humorous. As indicated above, the *context*—location, relationships and attitudes—must be right.

The key to the incongruity theory of humor is the existence, or setting up, of *expectations*, and the driving the action in a totally different direction. For example:

The Exploding Administrator

First administrator (irritated):   'How on earth can I understand this memo? It's been written by some terrible bureaucrat! Ugh!'

Second administrator: 'Wow, you're on a short fuse today.'

First administrator (gently):   'No, no, I don't have a short fuse. (Slowly, softly) I'm a very ... very .... calm person. It's just that (raising her voice gradually) when I come *into contact* with .... *Bullshit* .... (louder)...... *Yes, bullshit* .... I—I (suddenly leaping to her feet, shouting, demonstrating with extravagant body movements) ... **EXPLODE!!!'**

Here, the first administrator sets up the expectation of a calm, sweet rejoinder. Then her increasingly loud voice, the use of the slightly offensive term 'bullshit' and the extravagant term 'explode' create the contrast. This joke is accentuated by incongruous body language (leaping to her feet, explosive use of arms, etc). Again, context matters. Even a mild joke such as this could only be used safely in a situation where the two administrators had some familiarity with each other. A new second administrator might find the first administrator's aggression, mild swearing and loud shouting surprising, possibly even shocking.

Likewise, the one-liner: 'We're short-staffed today—but that's ok, because you're short' sets up an expectation of the meaning of the word 'short', then gets its effect by suddenly changing that meaning. And again, contextually, the joke might best not be used where there is a possibility that the short person might be offended by humor about their stature.

Incongruous humor is often about making a point by carrying a work situation to its apparent 'logical' conclusion, to a point where the words or behavior involved become patently ridiculous.

The Human Zoo

It is late afternoon after a grueling day at the office. The staff are tired and bored. Then the door opens and an angry dispatcher rushes in. She's really upset. She is shouting the odds about everything the office staff do—missing paperwork, inaccurate address lists, even typos in the email. Her voice rises to a frenzy; then, overwrought and unable to continue, she rushes out, unable to finish her tirade. No one else has said a word. They look after her in astonishment. Then Sofia speaks, 'This place is a zoo!' she says. There is a pause, then Gerhard, the group joker, gets up from his desk and says laconically, 'Yup! A zoo!' He leans forward, stretches his arms in front of himself, akimbo, and walks around the room grunting like an ape. They all laugh. Mike makes a chattering noise, like a chimpanzee, and pretends to eat a banana. Sofia becomes an elephant, stretching her arms forward together like a trunk, and trumpeting at the top of her voice. Soon they are nearly all involved, mimicking various different zoo animals with much-interspersed laughter until the situation is absurd by any normal standard of office behavior. Two nervous new employees do not join in, but laugh nervously along, eyeing the door in case an authority figure should come by.

Why do sane office workers do such things? Mimicking a zoo may be merely harmless by-play, but it could also be that those involved are using creative play to overcome boredom and frustration in their work (see Humor as release, below), and/or trying to make a serious point both to each other and to their bosses, about some deficiencies in the office system (see Humor as resistance, Chap. 9).

Thus, nearly all human behavior is based on some form of motivation. What is humor *for*? What is the motivation for it? How do people feel rewarded by it, and want to do it more? Here, we can add three more theories of humor, each based on a different view of the humorist's underlying motivation: humor through feelings of superiority; humor as a form of tension release; and humor as a form of sociability and relationship-building.

THEORY 2: HUMOR THROUGH SUPERIORITY

Some humor depends on the feelings of superiority it provides to the humorist or observer over those who are the 'victims' of the joke. The Colbert skit demonstrates not only the incongruity theory of humor but also the superiority theory. In the skit, Trump and Scaramucci are the 'targets' or 'victims' of the joke (not present, unable to defend themselves), while Colbert, in his impersonation and mockery of them (not to mention his good looks, smooth diction, mastery of body movement and facial expression, excellent mimicry and perfectly cut suit), appears effortlessly superior to them, and in doing so enables the audience to feel superior too (but inferior to Colbert, who they applaud relentlessly). There is therefore behind the banter a serious message (to Trump and Scaramucci): 'I don't like you, I don't respect you, I feel I'm better than you are; in fact we are all better than you are, and I want everyone to know it'. Such humor makes us, as observers, feel good partly because, by laughing at others due to their inferiority, we also experience feelings of our own relative superiority.

Using humor to put others down, or to laugh at their misfortunes doesn't sound very nice. In addition, it tends to run counter, in the twenty-first century, to the spirit of the times. Egalitarianism, the belief in the basic equality of all people, has been on the rise for many years, making it progressively less acceptable to render groups such as females, ethnic groups, the socio-economically deprived and those with disabilities, the targets of sarcastic humor (though powerful politicians are 'fair game'!). It is also increasingly recognized that humor targeted at individuals for characteristics such as obesity or shyness may be harmful to them. Respect for others is an increasingly stressed value. Superiority jokes can be seen as bullying, and bullying is increasingly frowned upon.

Much humor gets its power from making people look ridiculous. Sadly, we laugh at other people's misfortunes, even when the outcome may be humiliation, discomfort or even injury for them: that's why seeing someone slipping on a banana skin is inherently funny. The more dignified the person, the greater the contrast between expectation and reality (incongruity), and the funnier the event seems. This kind of humor therefore sometimes finds its way, in offices, into 'practical jokes', the archetypal one being the placing of a drawing pin on a high-status person's chair, or pulling the chair away as the person sits down.

Such jokes often risk injury to the victim and purely from a health and safety point of view are best avoided. Most likely the best such jokes are calculated to produce surprise and bewilderment rather than physical harm: we discus pranks further in Chap. 4.

This doesn't mean that superiority humor is always a bad thing. One form of humor which is probably less problematic is superiority humor directed against the self, that is, portraying yourself as inferior, even if you really think you aren't. Generally, it is much more acceptable to mock oneself than to mock others. Most of us have personal characteristics which we may acknowledge and use in our humor. Self-deprecating humor can be used by bosses to make them seem less autocratic, but if pushed too far it may seem forced and inauthentic and make others distrust the joker.

Then there is the kind of superiority humor which is directed not so much against individuals but against institutions. Ordinary people use humor to mock the inadequacies of institutions such as government, schools, religions, the tax department and others. Patients joke about hospitals, shoppers about chain stores, crime victims about the police, and so on. And of course, workers joke endlessly about the organizations they work in. Such humor may be damaging and destructive, but also change-producing and innovative.

The problem with superiority humor is that it frequently goes too far, with damaging effects. Quite apart from the physical risks of physical pranks referred to above, superiority humor may be deeply hurtful and damaging to its target person, who, in order not to be thought of as someone who 'can't take a joke' or as a 'poor sport', may conceal the hurt and pretend to share the joke, thereby encouraging repetition of the joke or even grosser, more offensive subsequent jokes. Humor can thus become a disguised form of bullying. As for the jokers, they may bask in the laughter, and sometimes the adulation and imitation, that their humor produces, and may develop rather too much of a feeling that they really *are* superior, to the detriment of their own self-awareness and realism. So there are psychological risks to both parties. We will have more to say about this in Chap. 9, The dark side of humor.

THEORY 3: HUMOR AS RELEASE

This theory, based in psychology, and particularly the psychology of Sigmund Freud, states that humor is used basically to release tension, giving us particular relief through the physical act of laughter. The theory notes that jokes often reflect 'taboo' subjects such as sex and race. For example, as we have confirmed in our own fieldwork, a surprising amount of workplace humor has strong direct sexual content or involves sexual innuendo. Are the staff involved working out their frustrated sex drives?

According to the theory, inner emotions that are normally suppressed can be released through humor and relieved by laughter. The workplace may develop norms that free employees from their inhibitions, and thereby becomes an arena for talking and acting in ways that would be unacceptable elsewhere. Laughter becomes an overflow valve for pent-up emotions, releasing endorphins, serotonin and other beneficial substances into our bodies, relieving stress and providing pleasurable sensations. The 'exploding administrator' joke (above), in its relatively harmless discharge of frustration and anger, is an example of humor as tension release.

This view offers a counterpoint to the earlier view that aggressive humor is bad because it damages the victim. Aggressive humor may be good to the extent that it enables the humorist (and sometimes the observers) to release uncomfortable or even potentially dangerous emotions safely: better to have inner aggression released in a joke than in a physical attack. Humor can also relieve the tension of darker moments: for example, waiting to find out if we are on the list of those to be laid off.

THEORY 4: RELATIONAL HUMOR

A fourth theory emphasizes the relational side of humor. While all of us think humorous thoughts which we may enjoy but never share with others, most humor has at least one humorist and one recipient, and much of it is shared in social situations involving several, or even many, people. A skilled stand-up comedian can make an audience of thousands of people laugh simultaneously, each one enjoying a *shared* experience, where much of the pleasure comes from the community feeling evoked. Colbert's studio audience and millions of viewers, even though they are spread out across continents and across time, enjoy a *shared* experience. Other television comedy shows have 'laughter tracks' added to simulate the effect.

Perhaps the underlying motive here is to give pleasure to other people, to make them laugh and feel good. In this view, humorists are therefore altruistic—their humor is a gift to others. Humor is often sociable, a form of sharing and bonding, a means of expressing and building positive relationships with others.

OTHER MOTIVES

So, is humor primarily based on incongruity, superiority, tension release or sociability? We consider that there is no answer to this question. These are complementary rather than competing explanations of humor. Each or all of them may play its part in the humor of a specific situation, as in our interpretation of the Colbert skit. The aware and alert manager needs to be aware of all of them in his or her pursuit of the effective management of humor.

But they may have other, additional, motives: by giving others pleasure, humorists also give *themselves* pleasure, including basking in their own cleverness and entertainment value. And humor helps its purveyors to build popularity, power and status in their organizations. This may happen without the humorist having any intention to do so, but some humorists recognize the power of their gifts and use them intentionally or even unscrupulously. Further, humor targeted at 'victims' may cause those people distinct *dis*pleasure, and may even be intended to do so. We consider humor as power-oriented behavior in Chap. 9.

HUMOR AS DRAMA

Barry the Singing Sock

Joker Mac kept a plain gray business sock in his top desk drawer. He had drawn some crude eyes on the sock with a pen. He introduced his creation to all his colleagues as: 'Barry the singing sock'. Randomly, Barry would appear on Mac's hand, whereupon Mac would loudly announce 'Barry the singing sock has a song for you all today!' And he would sing some nonsense ditty to those nearby. Barry also recited poems and limericks and chattered nonsensically to those who would listen. Barry sang and performed in a distinctive high-pitched voice that made most people laugh. When Barry had not performed for a while, colleagues would wander past Mac's desk and idly enquire, 'How's Barry, we haven't seen him in a while?'

Barry the singing sock became a pseudo company employee with his own identity and provided light relief and laughter whenever he made an appearance.

A last theory relevant to workplace humor is the framework-labeled 'dramaturgy' proposed by sociologist Erving Goffman. This view gets its force from the notion of 'drama', where the individuals act out their identities through their performance of roles, as a presentation to an audience. In the example above, Barry the singing sock became an actor in his own right, acting out the roles, and the humor, of his creator, Mac. In the workplace, the role may be not just 'manager' or 'engineer' or 'shop assistant' but 'big shot' or 'ordinary worker' or 'joker'. The role is a kind of script for the drama, guiding participants in the words and actions that constitute their 'performance' as they seek to impress their identity on others. Like theatre actors, each of us behaves differently in private ('backstage') from what we do in public ('onstage') when we are visible to the audience.

Viewed in this way, much human behavior, and most organizational behavior, may be considered as 'putting on an act'. The act each of us puts on, may, as we have seen, enable us to demonstrate our superiority, release our tension and/or express our sociability, but if we believe Goffman, it has much to do with what he called 'impression management', that is, manipulating the identity and status that others perceive in us. This is especially the case with the joking, banter, sarcasm, mimicry and audience participation we bring to humor episodes at our work. As we read through the specific forms of humor that this book describes, we need to bear this 'acting out' phenomenon firmly in mind.

Takeaways

So there we have it: the basics of humor are context; incongruity; superiority; release; relationship-building; laughter and, running through it all, *effects*, that is, the possible outcomes humor can result in, for individual people, groups and teams, and whole organizations. Let's summarize it, in terms of 'takeaways' for the busy humorist or manager of humor.

- In seeking to be humorous, or in evaluating or managing humor, KNOW THE CONTEXT, including the people, their issues, attitudes and relationships, the history of the situation and the surrounding culture.
- Be sensitive to the fact that context may make some humor inappropriate.
- Knowing the 'whys' of humor may help you to deal with it. Think about the motives for humor—of both humorists and audience—that you observe in your workplace. Superiority? Tension release? Relationship-building? Altruism? Prestige? Power? Something else?
- Be aware that humor is seldom 'just a joke'. By observing humor and people's reaction to it, we can learn much about them, about the situation they are in and about how they feel about that. When you observe humor, don't just enjoy it: watch it with close attention and see what you can learn from it.

CHAPTER 3

Humor Cultures

The humor theories we outlined in Chap. 2 are generic: they apply to all humor, even though we illustrated them mainly with examples from workplaces. In this book, however, we have a special interest in *organizational* humor, the forms of humor most commonly used in our workplaces.

In most workplaces, different individuals are 'thrown together', sometimes, it seems, almost at random, with the task of achieving organizational goals in combination with each other. We workers typically spend a lot of time together. As we become more aware of each other, we develop relationships—both positive ones such as friendship, empathy, mentorship, admiration, even love and negative ones such as contempt, rivalry, jealousy, even hatred. In any workplace, therefore, the common objectives that we all have to meet will be overlaid by a delicate, emotion-laden human network. And here, our natural expression of humor—our sense of the absurd, our aggression, tension release and sociability—will inevitably present itself, both expressing and changing the relationships between us, and often contributing to, or detracting from, our performance and our value to the organization.

ORGANIZATIONAL CULTURES

Organizational humor depends in large part on the organization's 'culture'.

Enter any organization and its culture will soon manifest itself. Just sit in the reception area and look for cues: the furnishings, the décor, the

© The Author(s) 2019
B. Plester, K. Inkson, *Laugh out Loud: A User's Guide to Workplace Humor*, https://doi.org/10.1007/978-981-13-0283-1_3

quietness or noisiness, the 'atmosphere'; the receptionists, how they answer the phone, how they are dressed; the 'foot-traffic', the people who walk through, employees, clients, visitors, what do they look like, how are they dressed, how do they talk to each other? Soon you will know whether the organization is formal or informal, urgent or lethargic, customer-focused or self-absorbed, and possibly many other facets of its culture. You may even be able to begin to tell whether this is a high-humor or a low-humor organization. How much laughter do you hear? What is the humor like? Gentle? Noisy? Bawdy? Perhaps even non-existent?

If you go inside the organization and become a 'fly-on-the-wall' (as we have done), and observe the everyday interactions of the employees over time, you will learn even more.

A Low-Humor Culture

Kapack: Law Firm

In a prestigious downtown address, Kapack occupies a stylish and obviously expensive building, which rises several floors to offer scenic views to those permitted entry. As you enter, you are struck by the building's clean lines, the sweeping windows and the beautiful polished wood floors. The atmosphere is calm and hushed, creating the feeling of being in a very modern library. A highly polished reception desk is manned by two well-groomed women, both beautifully attired in sharp corporate suits, crisp shirts and very high heels. These company gatekeepers must approve all who wish to enter: upon gaining the coveted pass card, you are escorted to the elevators and permitted to continue into the inner sanctum.

The work areas, you note, are similarly impressive, more functional and busier, but still very quiet. The floors are divided into tidily arranged cubicle structures, and individual cubicles appear to be shrines to efficiency and hard work, with little clutter. Computers and phones sit on clear, tidy desks, with a few sporting extra files and reference books. There are very few personal items: a family photograph here, a small picture or sign there.

The people fit with the businesslike environment. All are clad in corporate-style suits, the men wearing their suit jackets, buttoned shirts and ties. Some of the women wear skirts rather than trousers; most have crisp blouses or shirts under tailored jackets and their attire mimics the male suits, with the addition of smartly conservative heels, mostly in shades of black or blue. It's respectable—a bit like being in church. People type briskly on their computers whilst others, some wearing headsets to minimize external distractions, speak earnestly into phones in low, urgent voices. There's the occasional muted exclamation of annoyance or frustration, but no laughter—or at least none that you can hear. Overwhelmingly the office clearly telegraphs to you the message that, in this space, *serious, important business is being done.*

Would you expect Kapack to be a high-humor organization? Probably not, and our more detailed research in Kapack confirmed that you would be right. Humor tends not to be encouraged or to thrive in such a buttoned-up culture. There are no particular rules or edicts banning or limiting humor, and it's quite possible that at after-works drinks in the bar round the corner, or at the office Christmas party, the culture changes temporarily, and people relax more. But within the building, although humor might exist, it would be muted, almost private. We imagine two law partners conducting a quiet conversation by the water cooler:

Partner A: 'I see George is confident he will win his case.'
Partner B: 'At the fees he charges, he'll need a case to hold his winnings!'
They both chuckle quietly. That's about as far as humor goes at Kapack.

The essence of the Kapack culture is conveyed by the words, 'inner sanctum', 'shrine' and 'church'. There's something akin to formal worship in the way things are done here. And a common metaphor for misbehaving in a conservative environment is 'spitting in church': joking or laughing too much in Kapack would indeed, we suggest, be like spitting in church. Everyone would look at you disapprovingly, then try to pretend you weren't there.

A Moderate-Humor Culture

As a contrast, consider another organization:

Sigma: Financial Firm

Located in a small town, but occupying a smart high-rise building, Sigma has an official reception area that is formal, efficient and business-like. However, upon entering the cubicle-ridden office space, your eye is drawn firstly to a colorful and busy array of streamers, sparkly posters and banners hanging from the ceiling and walls, displaying a range of single words. These include 'fun', 'integrity', achievement' and 'togetherness'. These words, you realize, represent organizational values articulated in company mission and value statements. They are frequent, prominent and easily noticed. The word 'fun' is especially prominently displayed in several places, adorned with glitter and neon colors.

Individual cubicles are also brightly festooned, some with the same words and others with lively and cheerful paraphernalia including cartoons, pictures, photographs and ornaments in a vast and chaotic array. Everywhere you see color and glitter, so that the office almost seems to glow with energy and vigor. You feel physically warmer than you did at Kapack.

People are dressed in mostly corporate-style suits but not all are fully formal. The code seems to be 'smart-casual'. For example, ties are loosened, jackets sometimes discarded and while smart shoes are the norm, not all of the women wear high heels. Men's outfits are enlivened by sparks of color, with the occasional bright shirt or tie amid the blue, black and brown. Women's outfits vary more, from smart trousers and shirts to a variety of skirts and blouses, or dresses with flowers, patterns and colors ranging from soft pastels through to bold, bright hues.

It is busy and noisy. You have to raise your voice a little when you speak to people. Some staff, you notice, are hunched over their computers—opting out, perhaps temporarily, from the general bustle; others talk loudly on phones, call out to each other, exchange quips and jokes and wheel their swivel chairs along to join others in different cubicles. Some are clustered around the water cooler, creating a buzz of chatter and occasional gusts of laughter. This, you realize, is a busy and professional organization, but also an *informal* one, where fun, frivolity and playfulness are not only permitted but promoted.

If Kapack is a church, what is Sigma? More than a meeting, less than a fairground, perhaps a marketplace. There must be a lot of humor here, because you can actually hear it in the gusts of laughter. The colorful atmosphere and informal attire perhaps encourage staff to 'let their hair down', or at least relax more than Kapack's employees seem to. Humor is not compulsory, but it does seem to be encouraged. Clearly, Sigma is a higher-humor culture than Kapack.

A High-Humor Culture

On the other hand, compare the mildly jocular atmosphere at Sigma, with that at our next organization, Adare, already introduced in Chap. 1:

Adare: IT Firm
Located in an industrial estate, Adare's premises are small, unglamorous and surrounded by other small business firms. You climb up a narrow, grubby staircase which opens out to a messy room full of work cubicles and clutter. Two desks are situated near the staircase opening and these constitute the 'reception' manned by two middle-aged women.

As you look around the room, you can't believe your eyes. Covering the walls and cubicle dividers are colorful posters, photos, lists and—surely this can't be right—graffiti! Looking more closely at the graffiti, you find that much of the content is lewd and profane, one example declaring *'Bruce blows goats'*. The lists are of humorous sayings, one entitled *'Pithy sayings for work'* and including phrases such as *'I have plenty of vision—I just don't give a fuck'*. Artefacts include a clock that makes a flatulence noise every hour and another clock decorated with pornographic pictures. It is a shambolic space: amidst the expensive computers and technical equipment are dirty coffee cups and other litter. An office chair, broken and minus its seat, lies discarded.

Wondering what on earth kind of organization you have stumbled into, you are introduced to the CEO. There is a large megaphone by his desk! What for, you wonder? Today he is wearing a soccer uniform, but most days, you will find, he wears jeans and a T-shirt. The staff are mostly male, the engineers casually attired in jeans and

T-shirts, while a few staff, somewhat bizarrely, are more formally clad in suits and in some cases even ties.

People shout across the open plan space in this office. Frequently the shouting is abusive and derogatory but always jocular, and there is lots of loud, raucous laughter. People cluster round one computer when an email joke is shared. It's lively, noisy, irreverent and unbusinesslike, yet you have been told that this company is a successful and thriving business.

As well as a constant flow of vulgar jokes and insults, you will learn, there are many 'pranks'. These involve, for example, removing the screws that hold a chair together so that the 'victim' who sits in it will fall over, or soaking the chair's fabric so that the victim will get wet; having sacks of rubbish delivered by courier to colleagues; altering colleagues' computer screens so that nude photographs appear unbidden; signing colleagues up for dating or gay websites; and many others. The megaphone is used by the CEO to periodically shout instructions and abuse, startling everyone in the office, a ploy that is, however, greeted not with fear or obedience but with amused tolerance: the staff give the CEO as good as they get.

Such activities and artefacts are part and parcel of the Adare culture, and are enjoyed (at least overtly) by all employees, most of whom are male. And despite (or perhaps because of) these distractions, Adare people work hard and the organization is moderately successful.

If Kapack is a church and Sigma a marketplace, what is Adare? A carnival? A madhouse? A circus? A burlesque? Here, humor, albeit humor of a vulgar, sexual and abusive character, is openly on display, even to outsiders.

At Adare, humor is not just encouraged, it is a way of life, and everyone is meant to fit in. While we might think of Kapack as a somewhat repressive organization because of its cultural limitations on humor, Adare may be just as intolerant because extreme humor is more or less compulsory, even for those who don't like it or aren't good at it. Later on in this book we look at the scapegoating of those unfortunate individuals—sometimes labeled 'spoilsports' or 'wimps'—who may do humor at home but not at work, or whose idea of humor is different from that prevalent in the organization culture.

One other feature of Adare that makes it different from the other two organizations is that it is a small company that is owned by its CEO, Jake—a natural comedian or 'joker' (Chap. 7). Jake takes pride in Adare being the zaniest company in town. Jake wants to create a culture that gets its energy from his and his employees' humor. Having the power he has, he is literally able to create the company—or at least the company's culture—in his own image. So the location of power in an organization is important, even to the nature of the humor culture.

Which of the three humor cultures, Kapack, Sigma and Adare, would you most enjoy working in?

HUMOR BOUNDARIES

There are boundaries to all humor. Humor boundaries signify outer limits to the off-the-cuff remarks, banter or jokes employees are willing to voice. Everyone has some sense of when humor might go too far.

Workplace humor boundaries are largely set by organization culture. The norms of any group will set limits on what can and can't be done or said. And every organization, even Adare, has humor boundaries.

There Are Always Boundaries
At Adare, owner/CEO Jake, the joker-in-chief, took great pride in the humor culture and maintained that there were no boundaries to the humor. And when we interviewed the staff privately, many agreed that the humor culture was attractive, partly because of the lack of boundaries. For example:

'I don't think there is anything that is particularly sacred. There would be limits, but we haven't reached them yet.' (Engineer)

'The whole attitude is relaxed, and basically as long as you work, you can do anything.' (Administrator)

But despite their overall pride in, and enjoyment of, the unique culture of their company, some Adare staff were uneasy that total craziness can carry costs:

> *'I think, at any one time, someone is being spit on, so to speak .... there is a limit, and when the limit is reached I think the people are smart enough to back off, we don't target someone and bang, bang, bang ... we move on, the collective we.'* (Engineer)
>
> *'It's like knock your socks off, do whatever you like, as long as it doesn't hurt someone or ruin someone's day. It's not some sort of company limit, everybody knows how much humor you can actually do to an individual, it is limited by whatever the person feels, not limited by some sort of policy.'* (Engineer)
>
> *'Everyone has limits—girls more than guys— and the senior guys don't take shit and the women are safe.'* (Sales consultant)

Thus, even in 'no limits' Adare, there *are* boundaries: boundaries that, to some extent at least, protect members who have 'special' status, such as women and senior staff, as well as limiting the amount of victimization that particular staff members may be subjected to. These boundaries may still allow a great deal of latitude, and will not necessarily be sufficient to protect a sensitive staff member from the negative effects of the 'dark side' of humor (Chap. 9).

Within cultures, differences may exist. You may be able to share a joke harmlessly with your workmate that you would never dream of telling to your manager: it would be, as the saying goes, like 'farting in front of the bishop'. Like organization cultures, humor boundaries are both flexible and changeable. Much of the skill in managing humor—one's own and that of others –is that of discerning the boundaries of what is acceptable in a given situation, and keeping the humor within them.

Our research suggests that most employees have a good sense of their organization's humor boundaries. Our interviews with employees confirmed that most of them knew (and were agreed on) the standards that were to be observed. They were also able to identify incidents or instances where other members of the organization had 'crossed the line' or 'overstepped the mark'. Smart organizations know how to convey to their employees, formally and informally, where the boundaries lie.

Even new employees, quite apart from their initial orientation and basic training where senior staff guide them as to what the expectations are, usually have the good sense to move into the organization cautiously, not indulging in any behavior or words that might be considered 'risky' until they have become familiar with what will, and what will not, be tolerated.

OTHER FACTORS INFLUENCING HUMOR CULTURES

Size Matters In large organizations, the culture is shaped from a more amorphous top level, and is likely to be carefully honed over time in a series of discrete decisions. The boss of a small organization can decide, almost unilaterally, 'the way we do things round here', and take steps to implement it, including deciding on the types of humor that will or will not be tolerated and/or encouraged. Large organizations are likely to be have more formalized processes, more rules and regulations, greater diversity in the workforce (and therefore more chance of humor upsetting particular people) and an HR department better able to police humor if it threatens to breach company guidelines or get out of hand.

'Professionalism' is key. In most of the organizations we studied, professionalism was talked about a lot. Managers would say, 'We try to be professional round here' or 'We project a professional image'. It isn't altogether clear what professionalism means in this context, but it seems to be about orderliness, rationality, the appearance of being calmly on top of things. Especially important is that there should be at least a veneer of professionalism when clients or customers are around. Excessive humor, such as ribald laughter or off-color jokes, it is thought, is unprofessional and damages both the practice and the image of the organization. So organizations seeking this impression try to moderate their humor culture.

Culture Can Attract or Repel Staff An important factor is the way the organization promotes itself to prospective new hires. The 'way-out' Adare organization was well known in its industry to have an extreme-humor culture, and broadcast that image proudly (shamelessly?) to attract people who wanted more fun in their working lives: for the most part, such staff were very satisfied with Adare.

In contrast, the conservative law firm Kapack also tried to attract staff by advertising that it was 'a fun place to work'. But Kapack was actually a little dull, which caused disappointment and sometimes even angered staff who had joined the company with the wrong expectations and felt they had been misled. Perhaps the notion of a 'fun law firm' is an oxymoron because of the gravitas that a law firm requires, particularly when visited by its clients. To attract staff in this way, the culture the organization projects to the external world must be in line with the one it actually offers.

In our research, we met a number of workers who had left a Kapack-like company 'because it was too dull for me—no fun', or had departed from an Adare-like company because 'I found the way they carried on was stupid and offensive'. To some extent people shape and reinforce cultures, not only by the way they respond to the culture they are in but also by the choices they make when they move between organizations.

SUBCULTURES

Within organization cultures, there are subcultures. Departments, teams and other groups may adopt their own special variant of the organizational culture, or their own totally different subculture: the suit-and-tie men at Adare, for example, were the outbound sales staff, who had to dress according to the convention in their customers' organizations rather than their own.

The Power Rangers
Unicom is a large public utility, supplying electrical power to hundreds of thousands of homes. In most of its departments—for example, accounting, HR and marketing—the general organization culture and the humor culture seem quite normal—quiet dress, busy atmosphere, humor in good taste and so on.

But the 'Power Rangers' engineering team is different. These employees are almost all male, highly qualified and specially trained engineers. They work shifts so that power supply can be constantly monitored and secured. They sometimes have to don overalls, protective gear and tool belts. Alerted by loud sirens and flashing lights, they occasionally have to dash out to deal with emergencies.

All this has resulted in a totally different culture from that of the 'mainstream' organization. The Power Rangers' behavior and humor goes beyond other departments' bounds. There is more raucous, sexual and sexist humor, more tolerance of pranks. A sample joke asks, 'Why do women wear white at weddings?': 'Because they'll match the appliances in the kitchen'—a quip that might get the joker into trouble elsewhere in the same organization.

In group contexts, the idea of humor as a *social* activity (Chap. 2, Theory 4), one that pulls groups together in collective experiences, seems especially important. Humor provides an avenue for sociability, reduces social distance, makes members feel good about the team and provides a 'safety valve' for their feelings and frustrations (see 'humor as tension release', Chap. 2, Theory 3). Group members may use humor, for example, to (1) share attitudes to topics such as racial differences and sexuality in a 'safe' setting; and (2) express attitudes to the organization, its policies, practices and managers that they would not share formally.

Group humor, however, has to be developed carefully, over time. The length of time members have known each other is an important factor for successful group humor, and the acquisition of new members who may not understand the group's humor culture is likely to pose problems, as the following story shows:

A Clash of Values

Brenda, aged 48, joined a team of young people in their 20s, conducting sales and customer service by telephone from a large open-plan office. On her second day, she overheard Cathy, another sales rep, jokingly telling a customer to 'stop being a wanker'. Brenda was shocked, and gave Cathy a telling-off for her use of a swear word to a customer, and for her common use of similar profanities when talking to others in the team. Brenda thought she was acting for the best, to try to instill in the team a value of mutual respect and respect for customers.

But the result was that the team thereafter excluded Brenda from all their social interactions. Working in isolation, Brenda gradually realized that the vulgar jocular interchanges that she found offensive were in fact an important part of the jokey culture of the team and even of their warm relationships with established customers, and that the team was hardworking and effective. But it was too late. The team members kept Brenda at arm's length, and after a month or two of hostility and loneliness, she left the organization. Sadly, she realized that she should have been more patient, observed how the team's humor culture worked, and given the team more of a chance, even if she chose to refrain from bad language herself.

There are lessons here for managers, team members and newcomers. All should recognize the need for newcomers to be properly *socialized*, that is, introduced into the culture and norms, including the humor, culture and norms of the organization or group. This is a mutual responsibility, but particularly one for the group's manager, who might, in the case above, have briefed Brenda on the team's way of operating and asked her, even if she didn't want to get totally involved in it, to at least be patient until she had learned more about it.

MEASURING YOUR ORGANIZATION'S HUMOR CULTURE

Now, would you like to make an assessment of your organization's culture, focusing specifically on humor? Professor Arnie Cann of the University of North Carolina, and his colleagues Amanda Watson and Elisabeth Bridgewater have devised a questionnaire that will enable you to do just that. The questionnaire measures four dimensions of the 'humor climate' of an organization.

Cann and his colleagues were interested not only in the extent of an organization's humor culture but also in its *type*. From their review of the research literature on organizational humor, they identified four key *types* of humor and devised and validated a questionnaire to measure them. This research enables you to identify roughly the types of humor that you see as prevalent (or rare) in your organization. But before we tell you about Cann's findings, why not have a go at filling in the questionnaire for yourself?

The questionnaire is printed on the next page. We suggest you photocopy it and fill your responses in on the copy, thereby keeping the page of this book clean. *Don't* read on before completing the questionnaire: at the end we will direct you to an Appendix where you can figure out your results. Then we'll explain what the results mean.

Humor Climate Scale
Consider your current work situation in responding to the items below. Humor can be expressed or experienced at work in many different ways. Below is a list of statements describing different views about humor or the expression of humor. Please read each statement carefully, and indicate the degree to which you agree or disagree with it. Please respond as honestly and objectively as you can. Use the following scale.

Totally disagree 1   2   3   4   5   6   7   Totally agree
Enter a number from 1 to 7 in the space before each item.

1. ___Humor is often used to encourage or support coworkers.
2. ___Management policies are often a target for jokes or ridicule among my coworkers.
3. ___My supervisor believes that humor distracts from getting work done.
4. ___We enjoy laughing together about management policies we do not agree with.
5. ___If someone makes a mistake, they often will be ridiculed by others in the group.
6. ___Jokes about company rules are common in my workgroup.
7. ___My supervisor expects a serious atmosphere at work.
8. ___The humor my coworkers use makes the work more enjoyable.
9. ___Humor is sometimes used to intimidate others in the group.
10. ___My supervisor believes work is not a place for joking around.
11. ___My coworkers sometimes use humor to belittle each other.
12. ___Humor is something we all enjoy sharing at work.
13. ___My coworkers often make jokes about 'management.'
14. ___The humor used by my coworkers can often make someone in the group feel bad.
15. ___Trying to use humor at work could get someone in trouble with our supervisor.
16. ___The humor of my coworkers often cheers me up.

For scoring, go to the Appendix at the end of this book. You should have four scores, each somewhere between 4 (for a minimal amount of that kind of humor) and 28 (for a very large amount).

What do the numbers mean? Well, you can compare your scores with those of an independent sample of 572 workers tested by Professor Cann and his colleagues. Their mean scores were as follows:

Positive humor	21.1
Negative humor	13.2
Outgroup humor	16.9
Supervisor support	20.7

By comparing your scores with those 'norms', and seeing whether they are above or below average on each dimension, you can get an idea of how your organization appears to rate in comparison to others.

Remember, however, that the results are indicative but not definitive. There are many sources of error to the scores. In particular, your questionnaire indicates only your own perception. Others in your organization may perceive things very differently. To check the reliability of your scores, you might ask others in your organization to complete the Humor Climate Questionnaire (HCQ) independently (by photocopying the page multiple times and providing a copy to each one). If you take this step, ensure that each staff member completes the questionnaire anonymously, and that they do not collude with one another. You can then collect up the anonymous questionnaires, calculate their individual scores and the average scores for the group and decide whether any further action is advisable based on what you have found out.

The four dimensions of Humor Culture measured by the HCQ are as follows.

- The first dimension is called *Positive Humor*. In organizations high on this dimension, humor is used socially in a positive way, to support others and strengthen relationships.
- The second dimension is *Negative Humor*. In organizations high on this dimension, humor is used to demean and belittle others.
- The third dimension is *Outgroup Humor*. In organizations high on this dimension, humor is directed outside the group at another target, in this case higher-level management.
- The fourth and last dimension is *Supervisor Support*. In organizations high on this dimension, humor is supported and encouraged by staff member's supervisors.

Takeaways
- Your organization's culture will determine acceptable standards for humor at work. Think about this. Be aware of any explicit rules or polices on humor (some companies do have them). If you don't know them, take steps to find out. Just as importantly, understand the informal rules/norms of what is and isn't ok.
- Get together with some of your workmates and independently each fill in the 'Humor Culture' HCQ questionnaire in this chapter. Calculate your average scores and compare with the norms provided.

What do you learn about the humor culture of your organization? If you want, you can repeat this exercise for different subgroups or departments in your organization.

- Ensure that your humor and joke sharing fits the culture. For example, in a hushed, formal, professional office, a loud joke or prank is probably not going to please most people whereas a quiet quip to a colleague may work well.
- Be aware of how hierarchy manifests in your company. Do the bosses encourage jokes at their own expense and join in? Or are bosses more distant and formal? More formal companies are usually less frivolous, while more informal, relaxed companies usually accept more frequent and lively humor. Follow these protocols.
- Be aware that different groups and teams in an organization may have different localized cultures that tolerate riskier humor. Usually this stays within the team because the relationships can support this. Can you identify departments, teams or groups in your companies where the humor seems different? Think about ways to keep humor in the group which may not be accepted in the wider organization.
- Newcomers require sensitive handling. It may be a while before they can fully understand or participate in the team or company's joking interactions. Try to introduce them to the group's culture through explanation and demonstration. Give them time to work this out, and don't make them the target of jokes until they are well socialized.
- If you are a newcomer, pay attention to the culture. Understand the 'lie of the land' before you enter the joking arena. If you think you don't like aspects of the humor, don't 'rush to judgement': wait until the pros and cons of the culture become clearer.
- If you find the humor culture of your organization is either too 'tame' or too offensive to a point where it demoralizes you, recognize that you probably can't change it. Think about looking for another organization to work in, and check out its humor culture before you commit yourself.

CHAPTER 4

Doing Humor

The forms that humor can take in organizations are many and varied. It can be verbal and oral, for example, banter, joke-telling; it can be verbal and written, for example emails, attachments and display board notices; it can be dramatized, for example mimicry, parody, ritual and acted-out storytelling; it can be pictorial, for example photoshopped pictures, drawings and cartoons; and it can be physical, for example practical jokes and horseplay. In this chapter, we review some of the main forms of workplace humor and consider their special characteristics and their advantages and disadvantages.

CONVERSATIONAL HUMOR

This is the most obvious form of humor in workplaces. At work, people engage in conversation all the time. Much of this conversation will be about work-related issues—matters that the conversationalists are working on together, or comments they make on their organization or coworkers. For example:

© The Author(s) 2019
B. Plester, K. Inkson, *Laugh out Loud: A User's Guide to Workplace Humor*, https://doi.org/10.1007/978-981-13-0283-1_4

Dump That Tie

Russell arrives at work wearing a pink tie which he knows will incite comments from his colleagues.

He initiates this conversation:

Russell:	'I've got about 40 ties—I'm going to wear each one and get votes on which to keep and which to put in the bin.'
Dev:	'Put that pink one in the bin!'
Russell (to the others in the group):	'Dev questions my sexuality in this pink tie…'
Sara:	'Ray's got a pink one, and Paul has too' (Paul is the team boss).
Dev (grinning at Russell):	'Do you and Paul have a thing going on?'
Russell:	'I wish I did—I might get a better pay rise that way!'

But, particularly in breaks, employees will chat and gossip about their non-working lives: their health, their family, the TV show they saw last night, their latest shopping purchases, plus sport, showbiz, current affairs and so on.

In this setting, different people will use humor to different degrees. Frequently, such humor will involve mocking people or institutions that are not part of the conversation: 'I don't know where the design department gets its prototypes—I think they brew them in a cauldron like witches!'; 'The make-up lady looked like a scarecrow!'; 'Call him a quarterback? I wouldn't pay a quarter for him' and so on. Such jokey interchanges usually lighten the mood and provide opportunities for shared laughter. Occasionally the opposite happens, for example when the ridiculed person turns out to be friendly with, or admired by, someone else present.

Conversational humor provides a good opportunity for managers to gauge and to some extent set—by adopting a 'gatekeeper' role and making boundaries clear—overall humor climate of the group, for example

'I think we shouldn't say things like that about people when they aren't here'; 'Look, it's clear you two are always going to fight about politics, so can we leave your workplace a politics-free area?'; or 'Enough of the chatter, let's get back to work', while also identifying the group's jokers and other humorists, deciding whether their humor is on the whole more helpful or harmful and figuring out ways to manage them.

BANTER: 'TAKING THE PISS'

Our research across many organizations has revealed that another very common form of humor in workplace life is that known as 'banter'.

Banter is defined by *The Oxford Dictionary* as 'the playful and friendly exchange of teasing remarks', while to 'tease' is 'to make fun of or attempt to provoke (a person) in a playful way'. Note the use of the words 'friendly', 'play' and 'playful' to indicate the lighthearted nature of banter, and also the fact that, at work, banter may not be especially task related. But note also the implicit warning in the word 'provoke'. Provoke what? More banter in return? Laughter? Tears? Anger and a snappy riposte?

Some banter is so commonplace that it becomes routine. For example:

'Don't do anything I wouldn't do.' 'That should give me plenty of scope.'

and

'I'll see you later.' 'Not if I see you first.'

In many countries, much banter is called 'taking the piss'. Taking the piss focuses on the personal characteristics of participants in order to mock, tease or ridicule them, but in a friendly way based on affection and tolerance rather than enmity. Taking the piss often involves sarcasm or exaggeration. Although the words may sound offensive, they are delivered in a context of established social relationships and in a way that conveys goodwill, inclusion and warmth. Often, they are spoken with a smile. There may be an element of mock deflation of the other party, for example, by referring jocularly to something that the other person takes very seriously, or by highlighting the other's perceived or imagined shortcomings. Here's an example:

LightHearted Banter

Denise is an accountant known for her attention to detail, while Jack is a salesman who drinks a lot with his clients:

Denise: 'I'd like you to get this month's expenses form back to me—but you've probably been too drunk to complete it.'

Jack: 'Fill in another expenses form? Typical accountant. Even if was totally sober I'd need to hire Price Waterhouse to understand the details in your forms!'

Denise: 'Not my fault if the booze has made you functionally illiterate.'

Jack: 'I suppose you won't just want the restaurant receipts but details of every single item right down to the last lump of sugar!'

Denise: 'In your case I'll be happy if the bill for alcohol is less than 80% of the total!'

Assuming the right prior understandings have been built up, neither the negative stereotypes, nor the underlying aggression are likely to cause offense. For Denise and Jack are good friends who understand, and are comfortable with, each other's idiosyncrasies. Remember dramaturgy, the acting-out of roles (Chap. 2)? Denise and Jack are simply acting out familiar, and possibly much-loved, roles.

The implied criticisms sound angry but are really good natured. Rather than stressing the relationship, their banter cements it. And they are as likely to target themselves in their banter as they would each other. Thus:

Self-deprecating Banter

Denise: 'You'll have to do more paperwork on your expenses—you know what a pedantic cow I am!'

Jack: 'OK, give me the forms. But if I'm to face up to filling them in, I'll need to have a few whiskeys first!'

Most banter is like this: sociable, good natured, affirming and relationship building. Even if Denise secretly worries about Jack's drinking, and Jack feels that Denise's forms are nit-picky and time-consuming, they have accepted their differences, built a good relationship around them and use them as a source of fun.

The banter between Denise and Jack depends on the existing good relationship between them, and getting to the point they are at may have taken a long time and a lot of gradually-more-personal banter. In such situations, understanding the boundaries entailed by one's relationship with the others involved and their characteristics is vital. A casual remark which is taken in good spirits by one employee may be hurtful and offensive to another (context again!). A new accountant who didn't know Jack well but told him he had probably been too drunk to fill in the forms would get a very frosty reception, and not only from Jack but from anyone else who overheard, including Denise.

Banter as Drama

In today's open-plan workplaces, private humor becomes public. Typically, exchanges of banter such as that between Denise and Jack are not private conversations, but shared events where others in the vicinity can enjoy (or not) the experience. As we stated in Chap. 2, on 'dramaturgy', this emphasizes banter as a kind of staged drama, providing entertainment value for others, who may comment, laugh, jeer or even involve themselves in the drama as it proceeds. Participants like Denise and Jack may 'play to the gallery' so that the banter is no longer just between them but very social. Of course, for this to work, the 'audience' has to be 'in' on the personalities and the stereotypes involved, and regular participants in, or observers of, this kind of banter in this particular setting. Consider, for example, this next banter story not as a private exchange but as a dramatic entertainment:

'You're a Bitch!'
It's the tea break. Kara and some of her workmates are having a general conversation, when a voice shouts loudly, from outside the group: 'You're a bitch!' It's Alf, and he is pointing directly at Kara.

But does Alf's profane, aggressive insult meet with fear or anxiety from Kara, or consternation by the others? Not a bit of it. Instead, the remark is greeted with general laughter and a buzz of excitement, puzzlement and discussion. What on earth can Alf be on about? Still pointing an accusing finger at Kara, Alf complains aggressively that Kara, the organizer of a company movie premiere, has not sent Alf the ticket he has requested. 'No big deal', says Kara, it's an administrative oversight, and Pete will make sure Alf gets his ticket. Mollified, Alf leaves the group, but with a parting shot: 'Pete came through with the tickets, but you're *still* a bitch!' More laughter from all, including Kara. A few jeers follow Alf as he walks away, but everyone is smiling.

Gradually, everyone drifts back to their desks, still chatting about it. They've enjoyed the entertainment, and they're ready to get back to work.

What is going on here? Calling someone a bitch is surely insulting: why does everyone laugh? Well, sorry, but *you had to be there!* You need to understand the *context*. Everyone there knew that Alf and Kara are good friends. It would be hard for them to imagine any circumstances under which Alf would call Kara a bitch and mean it. Second, Alf's body language was a giveaway: the voice was loud and the words were insulting, but the anger was clearly feigned, in fact Alf was finding it hard not to grin. And everyone, including Kara, saw through him immediately, and hence the laughter. There was aggression there, for sure, but it was mock aggression, and there was also incongruity: the absurdity of Alf using such a word within a friendship and in relation to such a trivial matter. By making an apparent 'big deal' out of it, by adopting the conventions of theatre to role-play outrage, he was able to bring an element of drama and fun to the workaday world.

Banter is a workplace practice that helps people—particularly the 'targets' of the banter—to feel accepted by others, even with their personal idiosyncrasies which indeed the banter may focus on. To understand this, imagine being in a workplace where the banter is directed at everyone in the group *except you!* Or where everyone else's banter is greeted with laughter and yours with silence. You'd quickly feel rejected. You'd think 'What's wrong with me?'

Banter is where your mock-insulting and -demeaning of others is only possible because of your close relationship with them. You and they all *know* that nobody means it. It's banter, and that's all there is to it.

Or is it? Consider an alternative scenario for Alf and Kara.

'You're a Bitch!' (Take 2)

It's the tea break. Kara and some of her workmates are having a general conversation, when a voice shouts loudly, from outside the group: 'You're a bitch!' It's Alf, and he is pointing directly at Kara.

All conversation abruptly stops. There is a shocked silence. Someone interjects, 'Steady on!' People look with concern at Kara, who has turned as white as a sheet. She stares at Alf. 'What—what did you call me?' she says. 'What—what could I possibly have done for you to say such a thing?' She is close to tears.

People are whispering to each other, glancing at Alf. What can he be on about? That's not the way we do things round here—if we have differences, we settle them courteously, diplomatically.

Alf can see that his ploy hasn't worked. He never thought she'd take his comment seriously! He mumbles something about 'sorry .... just a joke .... didn't mean to upset you'. Kara's female workmates cluster round her, stroking her arms and offering her tissues. Others drift away in silence. A friend of Alf's takes his arm and shepherds him away: 'Best leave her be .... Just a misunderstanding .... she'll get over it'. Kara and her best friend go to the rest room to try to soothe Kara's rattled nerves and put the altercation behind them. Everyone else gets back to work, but no one feels much like working.

Here, Alf has clearly misjudged the situation, and assumed a degree of familiarity with Kara—and the others present—that they do not reciprocate. His banter has gone badly wrong, and has done so not just for Kara but for most of those present.

The problem is that there are other dynamics underlying banter that sometimes make it a risky proposition. First, even if the banter is intended to be harmless, underneath it may express some latent resentment or aggression which even the banterer may be only dimly aware of. Such banter may inadvertently take a more aggressive and hurtful form or tone than consciously intended. Second, the banterer, particularly if new to the situation, may simply misjudge the norms of the group, or the degree of familiarity and acceptance you need in order to be able to get away with something like 'You're a bitch!' The target of the banter may feel wounded or may have personal norms that exclude the language used.

Banter, like most forms of humor, is a weapon that can be used effectively, or abused with negative consequences. If used sensitively and skillfully, it can charm and engage coworkers and can express and develop good relationships and entertainment; but it can also, if used clumsily, wound deeply.

Often, though, the negative effects of banter, while serious, are not obvious. Banter, after all, usually creates the *expectation* of humor: you can see it in the bad acting of the banterer and his or her body language. It's as if s/he is saying, *this is funny, you are meant to laugh*. So people may feel hurt or offended, but they will laugh along with the banter. No one, after all, wants to be thought of as a 'bad sport' or someone who 'can't take a joke'.

In complex situations like this, the trick, again, for banterers is (1) to examine your own motives and your attitudes to the target person: if, for some reason, you are really feeling angry with them, then banter is probably not the best way to deal with the situation; (2) to be a good judge of context, to be able to know in advance what will work and what won't; and (3) to signal very clearly, through your voice and face and other body language, that what you are into is 'acting out' rather than genuine, even if this reduces the 'shock value' of what you say.

Another use of banter is to direct it at yourself. By and large, people like self-deprecation and exaggerated modesty by others. If the university professor who is acknowledged to be the cleverest in the group, announces, in relation to a mathematics problem, 'Well, I'm just a dummy who doesn't understand these things, but here's what I think ...' she is invoking Theory 1 of humor: incongruity (Chap. 2). Provided she doesn't do it all the time, it will probably work. And smilingly agreeing with others who offer banter about your untidiness or forgetfulness or arrogance is a good way of disarming them.

Canned Jokes

Canned jokes are a common form of humor across many social settings including the workplace. A canned joke is a humorous story, with a predetermined script, a setup that leads the listener to a particular expectation, or a state of puzzlement, then a punchline with an element of absurdity. Thus:

Two Canned Jokes
Joke 1

'A man goes to the doctor and says 'Doctor, every time I close my eyes I see a beetle on its back spinning round.' What does the doctor say?'
'I don't know, what does the doctor say?'
'The doctor says, 'don't worry, it's just a bug going round!'

Joke 2 (see Chap. 2, altered to a more conversational style)

A man walks into a Glasgow bar, with a crocodile on a lead. He says to the barman, 'Do you serve Catholics?' The barman says 'Yes we do'. 'OK', says the man, 'a whiskey for me and a Catholic for the crocodile!'

We apologize and agree, they're not that funny, especially the one you read earlier. But canned jokes seldom are, unless told expertly, face to face, in an appropriate context. While canned jokes are sometimes shared in workplaces, they are a form of humor that has usually leaked in from outside rather than genuine workplace humor. They are likely to have been heard on radio, TV, a stand-up comedy show or another social setting. They require a certain amount of skill from the joker, with clear, possibly dramatized, delivery. If the joker 'loses the plot' or delivers the punchline in the wrong place, the whole effect is ruined. Canned jokes probably seem funnier to an observer after a drink or two, which suggests they are better humor for after-work drinks than for the workplace.

Canned jokes are often raunchy and because of this the joke-teller, if he or she wishes not to cause offense, sometimes has to be careful to check who is in the audience.

Raising the Stakes

The Wednesday-to-Friday computer applications course run by the consulting company for the 12 top managers—all men—at Horizon Engineering had been intensive and tiring but successful. Everyone had mastered the technology and spirits were high. Now, all that had to be done was to enjoy the course dinner in a private room at an upmarket restaurant. The guests of honor were the consulting company tutors, Marie, Juanita and Gabriel. The food was good, the wine flowed. The managers were fulsome in their praise of both the new system and the skill of the tutors. Everyone was happy.

As the coffee was served, one of the managers got everyone's attention and told a joke—quite a funny one. Everyone laughed. Then another manager said, 'That reminds me of the one about the ...' and told another joke, this time with a mild reference to homosexuality, which garnered even more laughter. A third manager entered into the competition with a rather vulgar sexual joke. Soon all the managers were queuing up to tell their jokes, with each joke apparently even sleazier than the one before. The jokes and the laughter went on and on: no one seemed to want to do anything else.

The three tutors told no jokes. Gabriel wasn't enjoying the evening—canned jokes, sexual or otherwise, weren't his cup of tea. Should he make an excuse and leave? No, that would seem standoffish. He glanced at Marie and Juanita. They were laughing at the jokes too, but perhaps not quite as much as the managers were.

Eventually, after two hours of steady joking, Marie mentioned that she had to go home to relieve her baby-sitter. She said goodbye and left. Juanita and Gabriel soon followed. The jokes were still in full swing.

On the following Monday, back at the consulting company, Juanita took Gabriel aside and said, 'Marie and I have been talking. We found we were both disgusted by the Friday night joke session. Some of the jokes were horrible, and most of them were demeaning to women. We even think some of these guys were getting off on telling such filth in front of us. We're really annoyed with ourselves that we didn't tell them how we felt, or leave. Why didn't we? Social pressure, I suppose'.

So even canned jokes can be risky currency with the wrong audience; yet, as with much workplace humor, the negative effects may go unnoticed due to the social pressure to enjoy the joke. And, because they are usually decontextualized from the workplace setting, and require special skills from the joke-teller. They don't work well as spontaneous workplace humor.

Finally, in recent years, the workplace market for canned humor has been irrevocably altered by the Internet. Canned jokes can now be distributed effortlessly to thousands of people inside and outside the organization by email or on easily available websites. Jokes that people have heard, or read, previously lose their appeal, unless the joker can 'add value' though skilled presentation. We discuss the effects of Internet communication on workplace humor in Chap. 6.

PRANKS

Dictionary.com defines a prank as 'a trick of an amusing, playful, or sometimes malicious nature'. We have already mentioned the archetypal school or office prank of placing a drawing pin on another person's chair. The British TV show *The Office* had a running gag in which Tim encased Gareth's stapler in Jell-O.

Pranks are often spectacular and memorable events. If they work properly, and their 'victims' take them in good spirit, they can build collegiality and become part of company folklore.

Employee of the Month
José was a popular figure in his organization, and his choice as 'Employee of the month' went down well. Everyone enjoyed the presentation ceremony ('ritual humor', see Chap. 5), where José was awarded a trophy and a travel voucher, and he enjoyed the food, drink and good fellowship of the event. But the next morning he was astonished to arrive at work and find that everything in his office, including his computer and his desk, was thoroughly wrapped in toilet paper. As he stood there gasping in amazement, his friends, who had come in early to do the necessary wrapping, filed by, patting him on the back and offering further congratulations. And although now José faced the tedious chore of unwrapping everything, he was obviously delighted at the trick: 'You guys .... I can't believe you did this!'

This, clearly, was a prank that worked. But pranks have many downsides. They often take a lot of time and effort to set up. They typically cause at least momentary irritation to the 'victim', sometimes lasting distress, and often further time lost in 'cleaning up afterwards'. Sometimes they catch the wrong victim in error, with potentially embarrassing results. Sometimes they can result in feelings of humiliation, anger and even in injury. The most common response to a prank is likely to be mild anger: 'I suppose you think that's funny!'

Here's another example:

Hoist on Her Own Petard

Kasey was a small, youthful warehouse worker, new to the organization. Most of her workmates were men, and she aspired to be 'one of the boys'. So she entered into the inevitable banter among them in good spirits.

One day, quite spontaneously—'it seemed like a good idea at the time'—with much laughter, the men grabbed Kasey, tied her to a forklift and hoisted her in the air. Then they went off and had their lunch, only releasing Kasey after they had returned. Kasey admitted to us that she had been terrified but had not let the men know that. She needed the reputation of being tough and able to take a joke.

Although in the end, no harm was done in this incident, the potential for psychological or even physical damage to Kasey was clear. The joke probably also breached the local health and safety regulations, another important consideration in any physical pranking. The story also shows the power of organization or group cultures to move people to 'play along' with potentially problematic humor just in order to be seen to 'fit in' and be a 'good sport'.

If you are into that kind of thing, you will find plenty of 'prank' suggestions on YouTube and in specialist websites offering suggestions for workplace humor, including rigging chairs to fall over or fart when sat on, serving donuts with mayonnaise replacing the cream, layering a colleague's car in plastic wrap, and putting a fake body wrapped in black plastic by the garbage disposal. Other suggested pranks are so gross that we won't mention them here—we don't want to encourage you!

Prank websites typically include a commentary that advises you that however outrageous a suggested prank may seem, it will be totally hilarious for everyone involved, including the victim. We disagree: though most workplace humor carries an element of risk, pranks often have an especially high potential for unpleasantness, humiliation and recrimination, and even relatively mild ones may misfire.

The Wheelie Bin Prank

Pete found the routines in his organization a little 'dull and dry', so he decided to liven things up. He hid in an empty wheelie bin intended for rubbish. At a convenient moment, when his boss was nearby talking to some other colleagues, Pete suddenly leapt out of the bin shouting and gesticulating. Some of those present may have been amused by the pranks, but Pete's manager wasn't. Pete found himself called in to the HR department to receive a dressing down and counseling about inappropriate behavior. Pete felt terrible and vowed never to do such a thing again. He had totally misjudged his own organization's culture and simply hadn't realized that such an apparently innocent joke could get him into such trouble.

Again, it all depends on context and culture. Pete's prank was poorly received in his company, but would probably have been considered fine in the high-humor Adare company we described in Chap. 2

Compulsive, Never-Ending Pranking

At Adare, pranks were almost a way of life. Adare staff members vied with each other to carry out ever more intrusive pranks. Technology was rigged to display unexpected vulgar images. Unscrewing office chairs so that they collapsed when sat on was considered hilarious, especially if the victim was new to the company.

A 'fart machine' planted below new female employee Karen's chair and triggered from time to time through a remote control operated by the CEO caused huge merriment, and Karen laughed along with the rest, even though she considered the humor puerile. As she said,

'I left my last company because there was no fun, no laughs ....
These guys make me laugh. I want to be able to be a part of the
humor.... I would like to be a player in all that .... I think within the
next few weeks I'm going to have to pull some tricks from my own
sleeve'. A few days later, Karen used Photoshop to combine the
image of another employee with that of Mr. Spock of *Star Trek* fame;
then she put the photograph on display: a tame trick by Adare standards, but one that was enjoyed and approved of by all the other
staff, because it showed that Karen was learning what she had to do
to fit in.

There are, it seems, extreme 'pranking' cultures where any form of
practical joke appears to be acceptable—at least until it goes wrong and
someone is injured or badly upset. But overall, we think workplace pranks
are generally risky, certainly emotionally and sometimes physically.

Horseplay

The meaning of horseplay is conveyed mostly by the term 'play': horseplay
is lighthearted humor in which participants depart from their usual responsible work roles and play in an almost child-like way.

Unlike pranking, horseplay is spontaneous. It is also voluntary—usually
employees can join in, or not, as they choose, or enjoy the entertainment,
or simply ignore it and get on with their work. It is good natured and light
hearted. It is usually short-lived.

In horseplay, grown men and women cast off their regular work roles
and become someone else. We previously mentioned the employee who
described his organization as 'a zoo' and was astonished when his colleagues, clearly agreeing, began to chatter like monkeys, roar like lions,
and prance around on all fours.

Staff, sometimes senior staff, will sing, dance, throw a ball or paper dart
around, caper round the office, pretend to chase each other, play a mock
game of baseball, mimic each other or momentarily play the role of a
senior manager, or a teacher, or a jailer, or an idiot: all for the amusement
of themselves and others.

Garden of Eden

Boris is a telephone sales rep, but he trained as an actor when young, is active in improvisational theater and loves 'acting out' at work. He is also the established 'joker' in his department (see Chap. 7). When his colleague Claire pulls out a lunchtime apple from her bag, he spots an opportunity. He moves over to her desk and hovers behind her, rubbing his hands and licking his lips.

'Yes, yes', he says, in a soft, seductive voice. 'It's delicious! Eat it! Enjoy! It's the fruit of the Tree of Knowledge!' He emits a cackling laugh.

Some of the other employees catch on immediately. Boris is the Devil! Beelzebub! And Claire must be Eve!

Claire sees the joke too, and decides to join in. She turns to face Boris, a look of fear on her face.

'I can't, I can't! God told me not to!'

'God? You mean The Black Widow?' (This is the nickname for their manager, who is not present. Boris is contextualizing the humor as being within the organization. The other employees laugh.) 'Who cares what she says? Try it. Just a bite. You'll love it!'

Claire looks hesitant then appears to relent. 'Oh, all right then. What harm can it do?' She takes a cautious bite, then chews. Slowly, a big smile spreads across her face. 'You're right! It's wonderful!' She moves closer to him and puts her hand on his arm. 'Can I tempt you to …?'

Boris pushes her aside contemptuously. 'No!' he says. 'I do the tempting round here! I have a better idea. Get *Adam* to try it!' He points to Jamie, the newly hired office assistant, who is only 18 and is diffident and nervous.

Everyone laughs uproariously except Jamie, who hasn't cottoned on and has no idea what is going on. Claire advances on him, holding the apple out to him, beckoning and licking her lips. 'Come here, Adam! I have something for you!' Boris follows her, raising his fists in victory and cackling maniacally. Jamie looks both puzzled and slightly scared. Some of the other staff are by now helpless with laughter.

It is Claire who breaks the spell. 'No, I can't do this', she says, breaking from her 'Eve' role. She goes back to her desk and puts the apple down. 'Sorry, Jamie. Just a joke. Back to work, everyone!'

'Well, in that case', says Boris, also becoming himself again, 'put your clothes back on!'

This incident—perhaps a little more complicated than most horse-play—was a lot of fun for most of those present. It took very little time, and scarcely broke the rhythm of work. It involved no physical risk. It included a popular and probably harmless jibe at the 'Black Widow'. It may have helped to relieve the tension or boredom of a working day. It enabled Boris to discharge his 'joker' role and for him and Claire to enjoy the laughter and approval of their colleagues. It put a lot of people in a good mood. There might be a question, however, about how Jamie felt at the end of it: perhaps the supervisor or another senior employee might have a quiet word with Jamie afterwards, along the lines of 'Don't worry about Boris, it's just his way, ok?' But basically, provided horse-play is lighthearted, temporary, safe and victimless, we see few problems with it.

Takeaways

- Pay attention to everyday talk in your workplace, particularly the humor. Do people use humor much? If they are humorless it may denote poor morale or bad interpersonal relations, or they may see humor as a waste of time. Also, note who is 'doing' or initiating the most humor (see Chap. 7, 'jokers').
- Humor can be risky, so employees and managers need to understand the sensitivities of colleagues before jokingly insulting them or things that are important to them. Note instances of banter. Does it seem friendly or does it have a malicious tinge?
- Sexual, sexist, racist, ethnic or religious jokes are risky in workplaces and even at workplace functions. It is safer to leave more contentious forms of humor to the professional comedians and keep your jokes with colleagues fairly mild. Avoid topics with the potential to offend. Consider what action might be taken to discourage offensive humor.
- Pranks can be very successful, inclusive and can foster camaraderie. However, they can easily backfire. In approaching 'pranking', consider the organization, group and 'victims'. Is pranking a norm? Have others tried it before and if so what has been the reaction?
- Consider the possible health and safety aspects of pranks, the person you are pranking, and their sensitivities and attitudes. Also consider those nearby who might be affected by the prank and its resulting disturbance, and the possible reactions of those in authority.

- Never conduct or condone a prank that is more extreme than the most extreme one that has worked there, or that that might put another person at even minor risk. If you are planning a prank, check your organization's staff conduct policies, if they exist. Could your intended prank be considered a breach of discipline? If so, try something milder.

CHAPTER 5

Ritual Humor

The Omega Christmas Show

A retired manager reminisces:

Toward the end of my career at Omega Chemicals, a few of us, sharing a Friday after-work glass of wine, were bemoaning the lack of energy and team spirit around us. 'We don't have a strong enough organizational culture', said Joe. 'What we need is some *rituals* to bind us together'. Good idea, we said. But what sort of rituals? Annual dinners? Award ceremonies? Morning teas to welcome visiting staff? Been there, done that. Old hat, not exactly inspiring.

So then I made my big mistake. 'What about a show?' I suggested. 'You know, a few skits, satirizing the competitors and the bureaucracy and so on. We could put it on at the annual Christmas party. Celebrate the year. I've done some amateur drama writing and directing. I could ...'.

So we did it. I wrote and directed and compered. I dragged in whoever I could find to be the cast. The boss saw the point even though he knew he would be in the firing line. He funded it so that we could afford a few costumes and a pianist. He was called Wallace, so, with some trepidation I wrote a script full of Lewis Carroll characters, and entitled it *Wallace in Blunderland*. I cajoled colleagues into playing Alice, the white mouse, Tweedledum and Tweedledee, the Mad Hatter, the pot-smoking caterpillar and so on. The tunes were standards, the script and lyrics mocked everything Omega touched, the actors were barely adequate and poorly prepared—there was no time or space to rehearse properly. I was petrified. Would it work? Suppose no one laughed? Suppose someone took offense?

I needn't have worried. The staff had come to have a good time. They had all had a couple of drinks by then. They loved seeing their colleagues parading in ridiculous costumes or in drag. They laughed uproariously at the gentle mocking of our business. When the actors forgot their lines, they thought the show was even funnier. It was a huge success.

After that the show became—for a time—an institution. A new script every year. A new CEO who reveled in theatre and played, in successive years, Genghis Khan, Wicked Sir Jasper of the Manor and James Bond 007. A manager who admitted he had once been in a rock band gave a dazzling performance. An administrator turned out to be a trained opera singer. HR and Accounting people queued up to take part in skits mocking themselves. These shows gave me—and I hope a few others—some of the best days of my life. When I retired, we had done seven of them in a row.

The shows documented above were an organizational ritual. But when you think of the term 'ritual', what comes to your mind? Fertility dances or gift-giving exchanges by members of an indigenous tribe? Ceremonies of admission to secret societies whose members wear unusual uniforms? The presentation of trophies to the captains of winning sports teams, followed by speeches and votes of thanks?

In addition to these obvious examples, work organizations have rituals too, some of them much lower key than the shows in the case study. Afternoon tea or after-work drinks to say goodbye to a workmate who is leaving, a fancy dress competition at the annual sales conference, the presentation of an award for employee of the month—these are all examples. We believe, too, that in recent years, organizational rituals have become more frequent, more informal and above all more likely to incorporate humor, even the ones that are largely serious events. In this chapter, we therefore explore the use of humor in organizational rituals.

One definition of ritual, with the key points emphasized using italics, is that a ritual is 'a form of *social* action in which a group's *values and identity* are *publicly* demonstrated in a *stylized* manner, in the context of a specific event'.

Rituals are symbolic and collective: they symbolize community and what the community thinks important. They are deliberately attention grabbing. They involve participants having clear roles: the chair of the event, the presenter of the award, the recipient and so on. Rituals, for the most part, are organized: everything is planned in advance, and some of the humor is prepared, for example written down in a set of speech notes. And organizational rituals are almost always intended to be positive events, and so they almost always involve humor, whether that is pre-prepared jokes or spontaneous interactions prompted by the ritual.

For another example we return to our favorite over-the-top organization, Adare, whose zany and outrageous overall culture we outlined in Chap. 3. Most business organizations have informal and formal induction procedures for their new employees to welcome and familiarize them with their new employing company. Only a few will have welcoming rituals. But Adare, seeking to stamp its 'values and identity' firmly on all newcomers, had an over-the-top ritual to achieve that purpose

Karen's First Day

It is Karen's first day in her new job at Adare. She arrives bright and eager, well-dressed in a crisp white blouse and pencil skirt, her long blonde hair tied neatly back in a ponytail. People greet her warmly, show her around, take her to her desk in the middle of the open-plan office and allocate her first tasks. She types busily on her computer waiting for further guidance. Most of the staff, she notices, have settled to work, yet she's uneasily aware of the eyes of CEO Jake and other male staff covertly watching her.

After a short while a loud flatulent noise emanates through the quiet room and the surrounding males looked pointedly at Karen with disapproving frowns. She smiles and ignores them. After a short interval, the noise is repeated more loudly; again, everyone looks at Karen. After the third iteration, Karen laughs and says, 'You guys are trying to mess with me'. Grins all round but no confession of guilt (this is prank more than ritual).

At length, Karen leaves her cubicle to visit the nearby bathrooms. Her male colleagues swing into Phase 2 of their scheme, letting off a foul-smelling stink bomb which pollutes the entire office area. They race back to their desks before Karen emerges from the bathroom, wrinkling her nose at the smell. One by one they comment loudly, 'Whew', 'What a smell' and 'Oh dear', and from Jake the CEO, shaking his head, 'Oh Karen…On your first day here too!' Then the frowns turn to triumphant grins as the Adare staff fall about laughing and shouting. Karen laughs along as they also reveal the remote control to the 'fart machine' that they had been activating early. Karen quips, 'I'm going to have to dream up some tricks for you guys'. Gradually all resume work.

Then, at ten o'clock, the ritual starts. Jake has set up shot classes full of a clear liquid. Japanese Sake! He shouts—'It's Soju time—get over here, everyone'. Someone whispers, 'It's for the new girl'. Jake has laid an old electrical power cable on every desk. On his instructions, the employees dutifully tie these round their heads. Karen does likewise. She feels ridiculous and nervous. Jake shouts 'Three …. Two … one … and DOWN they go'. As an unofficial photographer pops a flash, everyone downs their Sake in one gulp. Karen, unused to spirits, gasps a little. Everyone laughs and cheers. Karen feels good. She has passed the challenge. Her chest burns but she feels heroic, and … well … part of the group. She thinks she will enjoy working here.

Note how Adare escalates the action, from simple non-ritualized pranking to a mock ceremony involving a communal uniform, a stylized chant, the ingestion of alcohol normally associated with bonhomie and celebration, a simultaneous action from all including the newcomer and a memorable physical sensation. The objective is, as stated in our description above, to make a fuss of the newcomer, to induct her into the identity and values of the organization, to make her feel part of the team and to provide bonding for the other employees. It seems to have worked.

HAZING

Karen's induction could be considered an example of 'hazing'—the practice of setting up ritual initiation processes where newcomers to an organization are subjected to various pre-determined pranks, and/or required to undertake particular tasks or ceremonies in order to prove that they are worthy of their new status as members of the group or organization. The main purpose of hazing, based on the findings of psychologist Leon Festinger, is that the severity of initiation to a group is strongly related to the group member's subsequent commitment to the group: the more severe the initiation, the greater the commitment. But in many cases, a subsidiary goal is clearly to provide entertainment, and in particular, humor and laughter, as established members observe the inexperienced attempts of the newcomers to accomplish ridiculous or humiliating tasks. In the United States, college sororities and fraternities are notorious for their tough and often sexually oriented hazing processes, and hazing has resulted in distress and injury, or even suicide.

Hazing exists—not necessarily called that—in many workplaces, but in most cases, it is much less salient, and the ritual element is minor. Mild hazing causes only mild humor. The supervisor may ask a new apprentice to 'go to the store and get me a left-handed hammer' (when no such thing exists), or 'go and get the report from Maggie on the eighth-floor office' (when the building has only seven floors). This is normally good-natured ribbing, and provided it is not followed by nasty leering and name-calling, there is probably no harm in it, and it does help the newcomer to feel part of the scene.

Adare's ritual hazing worked for Karen. It quickly taught her the key points about the organization culture, including the recognition that she too must 'dream up some tricks'. It made her feel good, part of the group. She was to find that the procedure, with variations, was the same for all new employees. Would it work for all of them? What about those who felt offended by scatological humor? What about those who thought the humor puerile? What about teetotalers? (If Karen had been unused to Sake and it had made her sick, this would probably have been seen in the Adare organization as a plus.)

Clearly the form of hazing used at Adare worked in this case, but it might not work in all. The problem with hazing, and indeed that of all organizational rituals, is that, being communal events, they tend to be 'one-size-fits-all', applying the same rigid process to a wide range of different personalities. The same kind of diversity in reaction is associated with our next category of humor rituals: 'managed fun'.

Managed Fun

Much workplace humor comes within the set of practices known as 'fun', or 'having fun'. Fun can be spontaneous, but it can also be ritualized, in what we call 'managed fun'.

Sometimes at work, a bored worker may say, 'Let's have some fun' or may simply start having fun, in the hope that others will join in ('horseplay', Chap. 4). When we have fun in this way, we are stepping into a new social space where the normal 'serious' rules of human or organizational interaction are suspended, and new, more lighthearted ways of behaving, including humor, become acceptable, even preferable. Fun is a lighthearted playful, *pleasurable* way of being. Fun includes humor but goes beyond it into, for example, pleasant informal socializing, conversation about non-work topics, behaving more warmly to others, enjoying music together, dancing, and perhaps decorating the venue (or your desk) with party balloons or greetings cards. Fun can characterize a tea break, or an office party, or even, as in the case of Adare, an ongoing way-of-life. An organization culture that encourages occasional moments of fun is probably good. An important point, though, is to ensure that the fun does not feel forced or compulsory, and that those who don't want to join in feel no compulsion to do so.

While fun can, in the right conditions, be created informally by employees and slipped into spontaneously, it may also be deliberately planned and organized by management, or a social committee. This is what we call 'managed fun'—the frequently humor-filled staff events such as parties, award ceremonies and celebration meals—often tacked on to top-team retreats, sales conferences and the like—that are sponsored and paid for by management in order to express and display their gratitude and/or to build staff commitment to the organization.

Many of today's organizations take the view that fun and humor are, on the whole, positive factors contributing to employee well-being, commitment and productivity, but that fun is too important to be left to the natural process of human interaction. Managers may consider that, if left to themselves, employees may either fail to develop any fun at work, or may develop fun that is feeble, negative, time-wasting, destructive, counterproductive, vulgar, over-the-top or confined to only an 'in-group'.

Instead, some managers think, the company must stimulate the right *kind* of fun: fun that not only gives the employees a good time but also shows the company in a good light; fun as a deliberate, managerial exercise in employee morale-building. Such fun may even involve bringing in professional funsters such as clowns and conjurers to help the mood along.

Typically, the company will sponsor the fun event with a major financial contribution, or even pay for everything. Among the forms of managed fun are organized after-work drinks and happy hours, office parties, excursions, food-and-drink receptions and celebrations, award ceremonies and organizational skits such as the Christmas shows mentioned earlier. These are all intended as fun rather than just humor, but humor is an integral part of most fun events.

Unfortunately for managers who believe in this kind of 'artificial' creation of fun, research suggests that, overall, managed fun is the form of fun least preferred by organizational members. Here, employees tend to be deeply divided. Some—particularly extroverts—absolutely love fun events, attend every one, enjoy the food, drink and companionship and become ever more committed to the company. Others—particularly introverts—find fun activities such as fancy dress, party games, drinking games, team-building exercises and treasure hunts childish, bizarre and embarrassing, and would rather not be there. This is particularly the case if the fun event is held outside normal working hours. They may be hard workers and good contributors to the organization but may still prefer not to have the organization intrude on their precious family and leisure time, but instead to organize their own social activities in their own space with their own friends, thank you.

Some employees may therefore believe that management efforts in this area are (1) venues for blatant company propaganda, and (2) veiled directives, with implied threats: 'You will have fun, dammit, and if you don't we'll be watching you in future!' The more that such 'fun' events seem to be controlled by, or oriented to, management, the more suspicious and resentful such employees are likely to be.

Karaoke Night

Lionel, the owner and CEO of the Tiger IT organization, loved karaoke. He had a good singing voice, was good at karaoke and had attended many karaoke sessions. He wanted his employees to enjoy this form of fun as much as he did, and he thought it would also help company morale. So he encouraged and funded karaoke sessions outside office hours, both on the organization's premises and off-site.

Some staff participated enthusiastically. But others shuddered at the thought. What, they wondered, did Lionel and the other managers expect of them? Was participation in karaoke compulsory? If you didn't attend, or attended but didn't sing or *couldn't* sing, would it be a black mark against you? So some staff who hated 'making a fool of myself in public', and simply didn't want anything to do with karaoke, not only attended but participated—and hated it. Others stayed home but felt frowned on and excluded by the enthusiasts when they went to work: 'Why weren't you there? You missed a great night!' Overall, the karaoke nights probably did more harm than good.

It's a natural mistake, which most of us make, to imagine that because we ourselves really enjoy a particular form of activity, then everyone else will feel the same: all we have to do is get them there. As the old saying goes, 'One person's meat is another person's poison'. Some people just don't want fun, or at least your form of fun.

This doesn't mean that management should abandon any attempts to organize fun in the workplace. Such events can epitomize the best that the organization has to offer, and can be used to build well-being and commitment in those who enjoy them. But managers need to take care. How can they make sure that their fun events don't do more harm than good? Under 'Takeaways' at the end of this chapter we offer a few guidelines.

ALCOHOL AND HUMOR

Out on the Town
The Triangle Property Group has a practice where a new staff member is taken out by several of his/her new colleagues 'on the town' and strongly encouraged to drink ten shots. The group always nominates a 'minder' to ensure that drunk people get home safely. Over the next few days at work, degrees of intoxication are gleefully recounted, with laughing discussions about whether the newbie vomited or passed out. The motivation is to create bonding and the emphasis on alcoholic consumption seems to be an attempt to speed up bonding processes that usually take more time. A key element in the process is humor: the workers consider these alcohol rituals to be extremely funny and especially enjoy laughing at the expense of the hapless newbie being inducted. Some employees who refuse or do not drink, feel excluded from the group culture.

The effects of alcohol on workplace humor is not restricted to ritual occasions, but is most common in those, which is why we introduce the topic here. While some employees surreptitiously drink alcohol at work, most organizational alcoholic consumption is done at after-work or away-from-work organizational rituals such as business lunches, social outings and 'managed fun' sessions.

Alcohol affects behavior and therefore humorous behavior. Alcohol acts as a sedative on the central nervous system. For most, the immediate effects are pleasurable: drinkers feel relaxed, confident, happy and sociable, though they may also suffer slurred speech, reduced coordination and loss of concentration. But it also affects—reduces—the inhibitions that keep our behavior in check and increases self-confidence.

While many people find the combination of alcohol and humor highly pleasurable, especially when with friends, it can be somewhat dangerous when the two are combined in work contexts. The double effect of relaxed joking and enjoying alcoholic beverages can change the everyday dynamics, allowing more risky ideas to emerge. The usual humor boundaries may be transgressed. In the warm, intoxicating atmosphere of colleagues drinking together, jokes that might not be expressed in the regular work context, may be let loose. It is prudent to remember that even after-hours work events and social activities are still work contexts and so work protocols and norms still apply, although some of them, such as those pertaining to alcohol may be relaxed for 'special occasions'.

While humorous alcoholic rituals such as those at the Triangle Company may indeed assist bonding, their overall effects are less predictable. How many of those who take part in such rituals really enjoy them?

INSTITUTIONALIZING RITUALS

To 'institutionalize' means 'to establish a practice or activity as a convention or norm in an organization or culture' (Oxford Dictionary). Would you like to raise company morale and cohesiveness by establishing humorous rituals in your organization? If so, there's no shortage of ideas available to you on the Web. Google 'workplace ritual' and you will find sites full of ideas. Here are the first few from a randomly chosen site:

- Celebrate wacky holidays and theme days such as International 'Talk Like a Pirate Day', 'Hello Day' or 'Left-Handers Day'.
- Create your own wacky theme days that connect to a work-related theme suitable for your workplace.

- Give everyone a standing ovation for making it into work every Monday morning.
- Have a hi-five day once a month.
- 'Third Person Thursdays' where everyone refers to themselves in the third person all day Thursday.
- 'Fishbowl Fridays' where you put everyone's name in a fishbowl and draw a name each week; the winner gets freed from the fishbowl a half hour or hour early.

Well, what do you think? How would these ideas go down in your organization? We're fairly sure they would go down like a lead balloon in ours (a university). The response from most of our colleagues, certainly the academics, would be a plaintive (or possibly aggressive) 'Why are you treating us like children?' On the other hand, ours is a large organization with many different types of employees, and there may be pockets of staff who would quite enjoy such rituals.

Our point here is that on the Internet and in some books there exists a form of advocacy for workplace humor that seems to consider that (1) it is up to management to organize the humor in the organization; and (2) everyone who is given the chance to participate in the recommended pranks, horseplay or rituals will want to do so and will find them funny. These reactions are products of what we call the 'rah rah' ('marked by great or uncritical enthusiasm or excitement', *dictionary.com*) school of organizational humor. The ideas may work in some contexts. But a key part of the management of workplace humor is being able to read one's staff accurately and to know what will be seen as amusing, and what will be seen as merely cringe-making.

ONE-OFF RITUALS

The Pink Parcel
Don was a maintenance engineer. He had his own little office, but spent most of his time around the factory. He was a professional, very good at his job. And he was an affable character, liked by all.

But Don's good nature had an edge. He was a smart man, and he could see when management wasn't up to the mark, or the union people were feathering their own nests rather than looking after their members. But he had no authority to deal with such matters, so in the end he'd just drop a word or two into the right ear, or make a slightly barbed comment. It was amazing how often Don's comments were followed by remedial action, without rancor. That's what happens when you're respected.

On Don's birthday, his friends in the factory threw him an after-work party. It was a good-natured affair, and everyone ate well and had a few drinks. Then came the presentation. The party organizer brought out an odd-shaped parcel, wrapped in pink paper. It was long and thin, with a round bit at one end. What could it be? Don unwrapped it, but there were more and more layers of wrapping underneath. It took a long time, and the tension grew, but eventually there it was—a huge wooden spoon, perhaps five feet long and totally unusable in any kitchen. Probably it had been handmade by one of the factory carpenters. Don was genuinely puzzled. He tried to say 'thank you', but what could such a strange present mean? Was there something sinister about it?

The organizer decided to put him out of his misery. 'Turn it over', he said. And there on the back of the spoon was painted, in beautiful black-and-gold lettering: 'For Don, the best shit-stirrer in the world'. His friends roared with laughter.

Don saw the point immediately. He laughed and laughed. He said it was one of the best presents he had ever had. And after the party, he took it to his office, and displayed it permanently on his wall, with the greeting pointing out Don's special quality for everyone to see. He was proud to be recognized.

Rituals do not have to be formally organized by management. As in the above case, any group of organization members can demonstrate their values, identity, gratitude, togetherness and positive feelings for a colleague by organizing an appropriate event. And normally such events will contain an element of humor because most people prefer the informal over the formal and want to lighten the mood with some laughter.

This example also displays a ritualized form of *banter*. We said in Chap. 3 that banter 'focuses on the personal characteristics of participants in order to mock, tease or ridicule them, but in a friendly way based on affection and tolerance rather than rancor'. This is exactly what Don's colleagues did to him in their ritual. If you look up 'shit-stirrer' in an urban dictionary, you'll probably decide it's something you never want to be called: something like 'shit-stirrer: a person who takes pleasure in causing trouble or discord' is one of the kinder definitions. But that's the way much banter works: it was because Don was so liked and respected, and because his little interventions typically resulted in solving rather than exacerbating problems, and because he was so good-humored, that his friends knew it was safe to characterize him as a 'shit-stirrer'. By pretending the negative, banter accentuates the positive. In this case, the banter had been developed into a full-scale ritual.

SPONTANEOUS RITUALS

Rituals do not necessarily emerge, full-blown, from the fertile imaginations of their originators. While they are usually structured, they are not necessarily planned. Apparently 'one-off' banter, pranks and horseplay (Chap. 3) can evolve into repeated behaviors, running gags and full-scale rituals. This is usually because the original event is so successful in amusing staff that it becomes a continuing or periodic event. The same applies to 'one-off' rituals such as the Omega Chemicals Christmas shows. If staff find them enjoyable, they may become regular events. For example, in an early (and classic) paper on organizational humor, sociologist Donald Roy describes 'banana time', a daily ritual developed by some of the workers in the factory where Roy himself was employed.

Banana Time
In the plastics factory, the men operated manual presses. The work was extremely repetitive and boring. One day, junior employee Sammy took a banana out of his lunchbox to eat. But before he could do so, another employee snatched the banana and taunted Sammy to catch him and get it back. Sammy plaintively begged to have his banana back and tried to chase his workmate round the room, but was unsuccessful. Eventually the thief ate the banana ostentatiously. All this caused huge amusement to all the workers except perhaps Sammy. The next day, Sammy once more took out his banana and the whole charade was repeated, the thief this time being joined by an accomplice: they tossed the banana between them to keep it out of Sammy's reach.

And so, what had started out as a prank became a ritual. Every lunchtime the workers would steal and hide Sammy's banana; Sammy would vainly try to recover it, but they would taunt him and would always ensure he could not get it. Eventually they would eat it ostentatiously in front of him. Meantime the group's supervisor/operator would continue to work, all the while chiding the workers and asking them for 'more production', a plea they never heeded. 'Banana Time', as the workers came to call it, occurred every day, always with the same script, arousing huge hilarity every time: they never tired of it.

Put in that way, the whole ritual sounds ridiculous and childish, and since it happened every day, almost as repetitive as the work itself. An important contextual factor in this case was probably the fact that the jobs the workers were doing were extremely boring. Much organizational humor seems to be generated as an antidote to the unpleasant, repetitive work that many workers face every day in their jobs. Humor breaks the monotony, and who could blame workers such as these press operators from breaking the monotony once a day by repeating a set of antics that they always found funny? While the plastics work that Sammy and his colleagues did has long since been automated, in today's computerized, routinized environment of 'McJobs' much work is similarly repetitive, and workers will often take every opportunity to invent 'banana time'-type routines of their own.

Thus humor, including 'taking the piss', often becomes ritualized, creating a constant (and comfortable) potential for the creation of temporary relief (Theory 3, Humor as relief) from the routines of the job. Such rituals look absurd to the outsider, but to those involved they may represent a lifeline to a sense of humanity in a soul-destroying situation. Such actions are, after all, something that the workers themselves, and not the organization, have created.

Did 'banana time' reduce production? Perhaps, perhaps not. But it is well known that such mass-production contexts—and some of their routinized twenty-first-century hi-tech equivalents—often cause not just stress but alienation, absenteeism, conflict, aggression, even sabotage, making 'letting off steam' in such harmless ways a viable and even necessary option.

Takeaways

- Try to list all the regular rituals in your organization or department that you are aware of. If there are none or few, or they don't seem to be much fun, consider whether there are some that could be initiated that might affect staff positively.
- If you like the idea of ritual and have values that you feel should be promoted, or people who you think should be honored in the organization, try to be creative in developing planned events, involving elements of humor, that value and honor workers.
- If your company has any form of hazing, we recommend that you err on the conservative side, and, if possible, try first to get to know a little about the 'hazee' and how he or she may react.
- If your company promotes a fun culture, do your best to join in with the humor/fun activities that you feel comfortable with. Be careful not to get too enthusiastic and go 'too far'—it's an easy mistake to make in a fun company.
- Before organizing fun events, do informal research to determine how popular they are likely to be. Talk with different groups about their preferences.
- Set up a social committee or group of trusted employees who can create and develop ideas for having fun and can discuss them with other staff. Modify the nature of the fun to suit employees' tastes.
- Promote the fun event as an opportunity for those who would like it but respect the right of employees to opt out and avoid any suggestion that the fun is compulsory, or that those who choose not to come are in some way being disloyal.
- Encourage different groups of employees to devise and organize their own fun events so that over time most people are part of an event that they consider to be 'fun'.

CHAPTER 6

Technological Humor

The Internet has changed work. Few employees in non-manual jobs do not have at least one electronic Net-connected device on their desks through which they can connect with the rest of their organization, indeed, if they wish, with much of the rest of the world, enabling them to do more complex jobs more easily and faster. Technology now enables us to transcend the simple desk-chair-office-colleagues settings in which business has traditionally been done. Even manual workers carry around tablets and mobile phones that enable huge connectivity with a massive, varied virtual environment.

As the workplace stretches digitally away outside the confines of our own little office, to distant locations inside and outside the organization, humor too flows through cyberspace and becomes available to thousands of new target or observer individuals. We no longer have to invent our workplace jokes and japes: they fly at us from everywhere, 'going viral'. Of course, digital humor loses that very physical, human quality that face-to-face humor has, but at the same time it can be framed into crisper, cleverer verbal texts and professional photographic, audio or video formats.

Just like face-to-face humor, digital humor can cause offense and distress. But there is an important difference. Whereas the face-to-face joke happens in the moment and then becomes a matter of recall and uncertainty, a technologically delivered joke is potentially immortal: it can be captured and distributed unaltered to the whole world and can be reviewed by workplace, or even legal, authorities.

© The Author(s) 2019
B. Plester, K. Inkson, *Laugh out Loud: A User's Guide to Workplace Humor*, https://doi.org/10.1007/978-981-13-0283-1_6

Daily, the Net beams in 'funnies', some of which have some relevance to one's work, but most of which do not. At the click of a button you can open a cornucopia of funny websites. Or, like yesterday's kids passing notes surreptitiously in class, you can silently share with your colleague a joke about your boss. It's easy to enjoy yourself, silent and unnoticed, attending to your screen rather than your work, escaping from the day-to-day mundane tasks for a few seconds, a few minutes, even a few hours. And much of this activity is involvement in humor. After all, humor is such *fun!*

CATS ARE ALL OVER THE INTERNET

Grumpy Cat®
With her own webpage and a book on the bestseller list, Grumpy Cat ® (real name 'Tardar Sauce') is an Internet celebrity known for her 'grumpy' facial appearance. She became famous in 2012 when her owner posted her photograph online and parodies were created and went viral. Her face appears grumpy because she has a form of feline dwarfism which gives her a comical annoyed expression. Her online fame has resulted in guest appearances on *Good Morning America, CBS News, The Soup* and *American Idol,* among others. She has been named 'most influential cat' (2012), won 'meme of the year' (2013) and received a lifetime achievement award from *Friskies.* She features in multiple Internet memes readily available on YouTube. Here is a small selection of bad-tempered thoughts attributed to her and presented in meme compilations, with the Internet versions including photographs of the cat in different poses and situations:

- *The worst thing after waking up? … everything until I get to bed again.*
- *Row, row, row your boat … gently off a cliff.*
- *Zombies eat brains … don't worry most of you have nothing to worry about.*
- *What doesn't kill you … disappoints me.*
- *I came, I saw … I complained.*
- *I had fun once … it was horrible.*
- *I don't like morning people…or mornings… or people!*
- *I purred once …it was awful.*

Why have this discussion of Grumpy Cat®? Images and videos of cats are some of the most viewed and most popular content on the Web. Cats are an exceedingly popular topic for Internet memes, and so this is often the content that is shared, circulated and viewed at work. In fact, when we were looking at memes of cats while writing this book, colleagues heard our accompanying laughter, dropped by to ask what was going on and eagerly joined us to have a laugh.

As our example shows, in an increasingly connected world, less and less workplace humor is shared in a face-to-face context. When technology is part of a workplace humor interaction, new elements must be considered. In this case, of course, the humor is decontextualized: the comments do not characterize a particular organization but are more about 'life in general'. It is easy to see, however, how generic humor of the 'Grumpy Cat' variety could be customized to enable grumpiness about facets of any organization. Because digital communication is connective between organizations and across society much workplace humor is about generic organizational issues such as autocracy, bureaucracy and loose ethics.

Online humor is streamlined and shared through technological channels or platforms and is readily accessed into the organization through a variety of personal and workplace devices. Technological humor is frequently visual, can also be auditory, can be photographic or text based, and may include artistic impressions, cartoons, sophisticated home videos or combinations of these elements. The Internet even gives us the ability to access forgotten favorites such as *Peanuts, Hagar the Horrible, Andy Capp* and a multitude of comic strips from the past. Here, we explore and discuss this ability to share all kinds of humor via technology, and discuss the pleasures and pitfalls of technological forms of humor at work. We begin by defining some of the newer technologically created forms of humor currently trending on Internet and social media sites.

MEMES

A meme is a popular virally transmitted image, video, piece of text or a combination of these. The content usually reflects a cultural symbol or social idea. Typically, memes are created to be humorous in nature, and they have been described as 'snarky' (snide and sharply critical) as evidenced by Grumpy Cat's ® examples above. Usually a meme is copied and spread rapidly by Internet users: often people adapt them and make slight variations. In creating a cultural or social message, a meme may be a curiosity or have shock value and is usually attention-grabbing.

Meme humor creates a sense of an 'inside joke' that viewers 'get'. Different memes 'trend' in line with other social activities and cultural developments. As memes become more commonplace, they are likely to become more sophisticated and perhaps even progressively more intellectual and philosophical than the current craze for funny cats—such as the range of memes found under the title LOLCats, currently featuring in many 'best of' lists.

A key to the popularity of meme humor is its brevity. Online attention span is short, and a viewer needs to be grabbed by the content in the first few seconds or they will navigate to somewhere else for their laugh. Therefore, long narratives may be unsuccessful. Trending and popular memes are often ongoing, with new versions being added to a thread which may become a cultural series of in-jokes. This type of humor is ideal for light relief in the workplace as it can be enjoyed momentarily, perhaps shared with some colleagues or sent on to others before the receiver proceeds to more serious work tasks.

A further advantage of memes and in particular memes about cats (or other furry creatures) is the safety of the topic. Although the memes are intended to be snarky in tone, it is implied that it is the cat who displays the sharp attitude. This is a reasonably safe form of humor, unlikely to offend many people. This is a key consideration when forwarding and circulating humor among colleagues from one's place of work. A cat can be seemingly grouchy and waspish without causing upset, and because the most common emotion people have for pet cats is warm, fuzzy feelings, the incongruity of a cat with a bad attitude helps to create the humor.

Of course, for all the cutely petulant cat memes, there are many others about topics that are less safe and more biting and these types have more potential to upset and offend. Memes can be racist, sexist, profane and offensive. For example, one popular work-related meme has hundreds of web versions with different pictures including one using a photograph of Gene Wilder as Willy Wonka. The text reads:

How to be a grown up at work: replace 'fuck you' with 'ok great'.

Then there is the equally popular but less profane commentary on modern work life with pictures featuring Steve Carrell from the TV series 'The Office':

When someone at work asks if they can fax me something.
Fax?
Why don't you just send it over on a dinosaur?

EMAIL

Evolving over 40 years, email has become one of the most common workplace communication channels. From the first message sent in 1971, email has become the most preferred workplace communication tool, and it is estimated that on average employees send and receive at least 100 emails each per day. Many workplace tasks are accomplished through email including work and personal conversations, and email provides a useful filing system for documents.

The dynamism of email explains why it has become so widely used; but users commonly perceive that workplace email is a private, person-to-person communication: in fact, it is often neither private nor personal, but a company asset that is subject to managerial scrutiny and legal implications when misused. In order to pre-empt the possibility of misappropriation of the company email system, which can create a multitude of problems for an employer, many companies create email usage polices.

In terms of legal issues raised by email, government policy in the UK and The European Court of Human Rights has decreed that employers can monitor or view employee emails and websites that are visited when employees are using workplace systems. Furthermore, email messages are considered 'documents' and can be used in lawsuits pertaining to work disputes and in claims of discrimination, sexual harassment and other illegal activities. All email messages can be archived and stored so that they can be analyzed months or years after their transmission. Such official use of employee email has necessitated the creation of formal company policies. All this should make users of organizational email, including those who use it to transmit humorous material, cautious about what they consign to it.

Typical company email policies outline that employees should not spend excessive time on personal email; that personal email should not unduly distract employees from work; proprietary company information should not be sent outside the company; and most importantly from our perspective, employees should desist from sending or receiving emails with potentially offensive language or content, particularly content that could be perceived as harassing or abusive. Such workplace policies usually allude to humor and state that humor which could offend others should not be sent via workplace email.

Thus, workplace policies often mention humor specifically and warn employees to be cautious with email humor in order to avoid offence. Specific no-go topics usually include racial or ethnic jokes, sexual, sexist or political humor, and aggressive or violent sentiments: more comprehensive policies may also refer to ableism, ageism and religious beliefs as areas of potential discord if parodied in humorous emails. This is very problematic as it is virtually impossible to accurately anticipate what might offend. Although some offense can be deliberate, it may just as easily occur through naivety or from lack of understanding of other peoples' sensibilities, belief systems and 'hot' topics.

Furthermore, traditional humor shared in person often relies on tone, facial expressions and timing, and these important cues are missing in electronic communications such as email, and so it is much easier for humor to be misinterpreted. With so much potential for offense and so many off-limits topics, it might seem that the only safe humor left is the type of inoffensive humor such as epitomized by the aforementioned LOLCats!

Therefore, workplace advice—and our advice—on using humor in email tends to adopt the maxim: '*When in doubt, leave it out*'. With the ability for emails to be stored seemingly forever, a risky email is easily retrieved and can be used to prove inappropriate or illegal conduct and even if the intent was to have a joke, the interpretation may be quite different from the intended purpose and therefore may become decidedly unfunny.

Email poses special problems due to its ease of transmission not only within organizations but also beyond them, as the following cautionary tale shows.

The PC Eradicator

Inspired by press reports on 'anti-PC' speech made by a local politician, Donald (no relation to the President of the United States), a respectable senior member of the conservative law firm Kapack, sent a 'joke' email to his colleagues declaring himself the firm's unofficial 'PC eradicator', who would 'take immediate steps to ruthlessly stamp out' any examples of 'excessive political correctness' sent to him. In an immediate response, another male employee circulated an email suggesting closing the women's toilets—'a hollow gesture of male compliance to the left-wing lesbian cabal ...'—and opening a men's games room in their place.

This was apparently a mildly amusing joke, and other employees, both male and female, entered into the controversy with endorsements, rebuttals and alternative suggestions. No offense was apparently caused. However, four employees thought it was sufficiently funny that they also sent the correspondence to various partners and friends outside the firm. The documents were further circulated and eventually fell into the hands of a national newspaper which used them to illustrate an article on political correctness. The newspaper also incorrectly named the unfortunate Donald as the author of all the material, identifying both Kapack and himself in the process. Due to Kapack's status as a respected law firm and its grave, traditional culture (Chap. 3), the Chair and CEO of the company were *not* amused but rather upset at the potential damage to the firm's reputation. They sent an admonitory email to all staff headed 'How a bit of fun can get out of hand very quickly'. No one was disciplined, but Kapack employees thereafter became much more cautious about their online sharing of jokes.

With all of these risks we might be inclined to surmise that humor in email has disappeared from modern workplaces, but this is simply not so. There are implicit advantages of using humor in computer communications as it can help improve one's likeability and reduce social distance. What has happened is that people have become more careful and use different devices and strategies to guard against offense and the resulting censure. However, employers and employees are still keen to enjoy some lighter moments in their working day. A decade ago our inboxes were overflowing with jokes: visual photographic jokes (such as memes), cartoons, text-based jokes replicating the verbal or canned joke (along the lines of '*three men walk into a bar...*'), but recent research shows that more recently this behavior has declined.

Somewhere along the way, probably around the time that email became recognized as official workplace documentation, the enthusiastic and sometimes excessive sharing of jokes gradually reduced and declined. People became more aware of the pitfalls, and so some people simply stopped sending any email humor, while others stopped sending their jokes to their entire address list and instead now select much more carefully which joke to send to which recipient. Such selectivity requires knowledge of coworkers that includes those who might appreciate a certain type of joke and those who will not: those whose potential reactions are unknown are better left off the circulation list. All this seems to us to signal a 'growing up' of the medium and more sophistication in those using it, with a more comprehensive understanding of the potential power, distribution and longevity of jokes sent in email.

Emoji ☺

Alongside this deepening knowledge of the implications of email humor has come the development of visual devices to enhance our email communications. Emoji (and emoticons) were invented to lighten or mitigate electronic messages by visually indicating and showing that the author is either joking, lighthearted, or at least not intending a harsh tone.

Emoji are sometimes confounded with **'emoticons'**, and although there are subtle differences they are often treated as the same thing. To briefly explain, an *'emoticon'* is a typographic display of a facial representation and is used to show emotion in text-based mediums such as in a text message sent on a smartphone or more usually in an email. This is a common example of an emoticon ☺ which is created by using a full colon ☺ and a bracket. This smiley emoticon was the first 'grassroots' creation to show emotion in text.

In contrast, *emoji* were created in the late 1990s by a Japanese communications firm. Basically, the word means 'pictograph', and these graphic devices are actual pictures that can be inserted into text to portray emotion. Emoji are extensions to the typographical characters used by most operating systems today and are casually added to enhance text messages (also called Short Message Services—SMS). Emoji are now found in most modern communication apps such as smartphone text messaging and are imbedded into social networking applications such as Facebook, Instagram, Twitter, and Snapchat. There are also *'stickers'* which are customized pictures used in some of the instant messaging applications such as Facebook Messenger. These are sometimes referred to as emoji, but these are specific to the application and cannot be used elsewhere.

The advantage of emoji is that this small digital image or icon can be used to express an emotion in electronic communication. It can liven up your text messages and act as a proxy for the body language component that is absent in electronic communication. Emoji stand in for gestures, facial expressions, tone, which can help understanding, especially of intent. They are easy to use and can add a personal connection in electronic communications. This is really useful when you want to ensure that the recipient of a message knows that you are teasing, lighthearted or sarcastic—all of which is difficult to convey when you are not physically present. A smiley face with a wink easily conveys, we're just joking ☺.

There is even an online 'emojipedia' where a search on the term *laugh* results in five emoji including rolling on the floor laughing; face with tears of joy; smiling face with closed eyes and open mouth; cat face; cat face with tears of joy (as claimed at the start of the chapter, cats are everywhere on the Web).

With so many emoji readily available it is easy to overdo their use, 😨 and they are still somewhat 'frowned upon' in some formal work communications, but they are becoming increasingly more accepted as our electronic communication pervades work and life. Our recommendation is to use them sparingly and wisely and of course always consider the context. After all, a *'roll on the floor laughing'* (ROFL) emoji is not going to be appreciated on an email discussing organizational issues such as downsizing, retrenching or restructuring.

SOCIAL MEDIA

Humor is highly popular and desirable in social networking domains, and humor can enhance Internet experiences with quick hooks and one-liner comic moments. Such comic Internet activities promote being 'on trend', and those who create or are early sharers of the latest viral jokes may achieve high status in the online environment. Those in the know about the latest comic GIFS, memes, and mash-ups may experience the satisfying warmth of being in the 'in-group' and au fait with the 'in jokes'.

It seems quite feasible that connected adults now tell fewer face-to-face jokes, and humor researchers have speculated that the 2001 World Trade Centre attacks were catalysts for a new genre of 'disaster jokes' expressed through text and image and widely circulated via the Internet and social networking sites (SNSs). With content constantly added, altered and updated by users, the Internet is a massive archive for comic and humor performances, snippets, skits and cartoons from the past and present.

Such a treasury of humor may be irresistible for workers. A quick search for content that amuses can offer a pleasurable microbreak and relief from work pressure. As so much is readily available online, it is not apparent whether an employee is working hard on an important file or enjoying the latest meme on their screen. Of course, their wide grin or loud laugh may give them away: 'cyberloafing' (or 'cyberslacking') is a real and researched modern workplace issue purportedly costing companies billions of dollars in lost revenue. Once something amusing is found, a simple click or two allows the errant worker to share, post or forward the content to a few particular people or to everyone in their social network. Humor circulates very quickly this way, and popular trending jokes may appear and reappear in various domains, shared by many of your contacts and friends as they gain momentum and 'go viral'.

One of the key issues with SNSs is the blurring of the boundary between the work domain and other 'life' domains. Our worker, ostensibly working hard but in reality posting funny memes on SNSs can reach friends and family outside of work as well as coworkers and managers inside work. It is becoming increasingly hard to separate the work and social domains, and this causes some new issues and has implications for humor sharing. For example, our meme-loving worker has likely created an online profile in his or her favored SNS. It is likely that he/she has shared information about life, work, interests and connections. Many people name the organizations that they work for as this is often a significant aspect of their identity.

They may then decide to share a joke that they find highly amusing; but to others it may be offensive or profane. Workers may share jokes via their personal SNS: but when their personal sharing is linked with their organizational affiliation their employing company can claim that their personal posting, even though jocular, has brought the company into disrepute. This has become a common problem, so much so that some people create multiple profiles, while others find ways of adjusting privacy settings to limit who might see their post.

It's usually a dilemma whether or not to add your boss as a friend on Facebook. Privacy measures can only limit exposure to a certain degree because anything posted online can be captured in multiple ways and recirculated to those who may not have been privy to the initial post. This has been the case in some high-profile workplace SNS 'fails':

Letting the Company in on the Joke

In 2009, Connor Riley (22) was offered a job by Cisco. Trying to be lightly amusing, she tweeted: 'Cisco just offered me a job! Now I have to weigh the utility of a fatty paycheck against the daily commute to San José and hating the work'. Bur Connor had forgotten to keep her worldwide tweet private. It was sent to someone in the Cisco company, and the job offer was retracted.

In 2012, a call center employee in Northern Ireland posted jocular derogatory comments about a coworker's sexual activities on Facebook. He did so from his own home, after work, while under the influence of alcohol. He claimed that he was 'just taking the piss' and that the coworker had taken his remarks too seriously. Although his intention was to joke, the disparaging comments were considered to be harassment and caused distress. His subsequent dismissal was deemed to be legal and fair.

Although these are fairly old cases now, there are still work dismissals that occur from social media posts, and humor is often a dimension of problematic posting.

These examples highlight some of the pitfalls of posting jokes about work contexts on SNSs and the likelihood of causing offence. They also exemplify that in such overt, highly connected forums, claiming 'just joking' as a defense is not a 'get-out-of jail-free' card especially when the joking is derogatory and harmful.

CONCLUDING COMMENTS

As with many of our social behaviors, humor has had to adapt to different contexts, mediums, forms and styles. Although humor is a significant feature of technological interactions, it must, like face-to-face joking and banter, be used with care and sensitivity. Because the potential for wider circulation and thus greater outrage is immense, it may need even more care. The blurring of boundaries between social and work domains enabled by social media adds another layer of complexity that needs to be considered in online joking.

This chapter has highlighted some modern media for, and conventions of, humor as well as emerging issues for sharing humor in and about work and workers. Technology is advancing so rapidly that some researchers have even found it necessary to investigate responses to jokes when delivered by robots and Artificial Intelligence (AI) is going to have new and different impacts that we can only begin to try and anticipate.

We can be sure that our technologically capable work will continue to change rapidly. We will need our sense of humor to help us cope with work, technology and change, but who knows what form our joking and laughter will adopt next? Hopefully it will be fun finding out.

We'll let Grumpy cat and the LOLCats have the last word:

GC: *'Every day I spend at work…Is the worst day ever'.*
LOLCats: *'I work from home…I don't have to wear my happy face'.*

Takeaways
We note that these takeaways are equally relevant to both managers and workers, in other words, to everyone at work. Therefore, we suggest that this list might be used by managers to share and discuss e-humor with their subordinate colleagues to develop some shared protocols in workplaces.

- It is safest to ensure that any jokes or humor shared through e-channels do not have racial, ethnic, sexual, sexist, political, religious or violent themes or content. This might limit your scope, but electronic sources can be used as legal documents if complaints arise—so care is advised.
- Similarly, take care in who you send jokes to and where you post. Some people disapprove of any jokes sent to them electronically at work, so know your recipients. 'Send all' is never a good idea in humor sharing.
- Emoticons and emoji can be useful tools in e-messages but use sparingly and judiciously. Do not use at all in highly formal communications such as disciplinary documents.
- Be careful with the content that you display on your screen. Visual jokes may cause offense or be misconstrued. Keep in mind that open-plan offices are very public space, so open joke files with caution or not at all if you're worried about the content.
- If your social media presence is associated with your organization or accessible to colleagues and bosses, then consider carefully what you

post and keep the same parameters for humor that we have outlined in this and other chapters.

- Even when posting jokes outside of work hours, consider: How would I feel if my boss/ colleague/ apprentice/ junior /CEO/ mentor saw this joke I am posting?
- A useful rule of thumb may be to consider how you would feel if your joke was front page news and attributed to you. If it would make you uncomfortable then perhaps don't post/send it.

CHAPTER 7

Jokers Wild!

Mac the Life

If you ask people in the Bytes Company, 'who is the 'joker' round here?' they all give the same answer, point to the same man: Mac.

Mac is a systems analyst. He is in his mid-forties and is physically distinctive: a large paunch, thick dark hair and a goatee beard. He is English.

Mac might be described as 'the life and soul of the party'. He has a booming voice. His jokes and quips are delivered in the open-plan office space where everyone can hear him. His distinctive English accent somehow seems to make his declamations sound even funnier. Much of his joking is at his own expense. As Mac says, 'You share a lot of yourself in joking'. Jokers aren't shy, and shy people don't become jokers.

But Mac's comedy is more than just funny remarks—it is a series of *performances*, to a largely supportive audience of his coworkers, whose members laugh and sometimes applaud. In Chap. 2, we mentioned Mac's invented character 'Barry the singing sock': a sock puppet through whom Mac relays songs, limericks and other nonsense. Mac loves acting the fool. One Friday morning before an avidly anticipated football match involving his beloved England team, Mac loudly informs everyone that he will be spending all weekend naked but for a large Union Jack flag. 'EWWW!' chorus his

© The Author(s) 2019
B. Plester, K. Inkson, *Laugh out Loud: A User's Guide to Workplace Humor*, https://doi.org/10.1007/978-981-13-0283-1_7

colleagues, roaring with laughter. Not funny? You had to be there! You had to know and understand Mac!

Mac sees his joker role as being for everybody. No one escapes. When his colleague Joe celebrates his 40th birthday, Mac loudly declares that Joe now 'looks like his dad'. When a new woman joins the team Mac is heard loudly asking, within her hearing, 'How soon can we start teasing the new girl?' According to Mac, 'I encourage people to laugh, even those you wouldn't think would enjoy it. I try to involve everyone around, so I wander around a lot. Everyone without exception gets ragged or ribbed'.

Mac 'pushes the boundaries' of what is acceptable. As he says, 'I can't afford to be too PC (politically correct). Some of the stuff I do is a bit borderline, but I'm not perverted or lusting after anyone and usually it's not taken the wrong way. Sometimes I say things for shock value'. When a male colleague arrives at work with a brightly colored shirt on, Mac loudly announces to the room, 'I see it's gay shirt day!'—a joke with a potential slur about gay people. He calls a recent immigrant colleague 'fresh off the boat', to which she retorts, 'you're just a pommie* fat white boy': they both laugh uproariously.

In a signature joke, Mac will perform a 'tummy bang' with another (similarly paunchy) male staff member: they run towards each other and bang their stomachs together. This can startle newcomers or visitors but causes huge laughter in the office; indeed sometimes, when the office is quiet, colleagues even call for a tummy bang.

Mac is revered by his colleagues for his humor. But what of his managers? They acknowledge that such a joker is great for morale but are nervous about some of his joking. Perhaps one day he will go too far.

*Australasian slang for immigrant English people.

Mac is a humorist, an individual organizational member who consciously and consistently creates, and is a central focus for, humor in his workplace. Nearly every work setting has one or more jokers, and normally most people will agree who the joker is. Note Mac's characteristics: quick-witted, extroverted, sociable, 'look at me' showing-off and willingness to take minor personal risks.

Some people maintain that jokers are not only inevitable in social settings but essential. If we go back to medieval times, royal courts actually appointed jokers—then known as court jesters, or fools—to provide amusement and entertainment to the monarch and nobles. Whereas in many social situations being humorous is considered an 'optional extra', court jesters were *expected* to quip, jest and otherwise act the fool: the equivalent of today's stand-up comedians, but released from the stage to perform in everyday settings. The main difference between court jesters and workplace jokers is that whereas the jesters were formally appointed to their positions (and even given droll, multicolored costumes to signify their special status), workplace jokers tend to 'take on' their special role by gradually imposing their humor on the situation until their position is informally recognized by all.

Notably, court jesters, even though they were typically low born, were given special privilege to tease and abuse the nobility who employed them. Take this exchange from Shakespeare's *Twelfth Night,* as the humble jester 'winds up' the aristocratic Olivia:

Fool: 'My dear madam, why are you in mourning?'
Olivia: 'My dear fool, because my brother died.'
Fool: 'I think his soul's in hell, my lady.'
Olivia: 'I know his soul's in heaven, fool.'
Fool: 'Then you're a fool for being sad that your brother's soul is in heaven. Take away this fool, gentlemen!'

The jester's license to say things that might be considered rude, even treasonous, to his monarch-employer is paralleled today by jokers' implicit permission to 'push the boundaries', for example to use irony and sarcasm—'dark humor'—to say things that other people might think, but would not dare to say.

Every Silver Lining Has a Cloud
It's Clearview Products' monthly sales meeting. The Sales Manager is finishing his report of the previous month's figures. It's terrible. Everyone's sales are down. A competitor has brought out a new product which is beating their own hands-down in the marketplace. Two big orders have been returned due to faulty components. Management is worried about the future of the company.

'But', concludes the sales manager, 'we have been through worse than this before. We have a strong product line, you are a great team, and I know you will work even harder to turn this around. If we all put our shoulders to the wheel, support each other through a difficult time and above all believe in ourselves, believe in the company, by this time next year we will be congratulating ourselves on our best sales year ever. ... Now, are there any questions?'

There is a long, depressed, pregnant pause. Then, at the back, the joker rises to his feet and clears his throat.

'I have a question.'

'Yes?'

'Can we all rely on you for a good reference?'

The tension is broken. Everyone laughs, including the sales manager, who waits for the laughter to die down, then says, 'Look, I hear what you're saying. It's really not as bad as that, but since you ask, here's the company's view about downsizing ...'.

Here, the joker has used dark humor to voice a fear that everyone may be thinking, but that most would never state. The humor is exaggerated by the contrast of the joker's irony with the manager's upbeat cheerleading. Everyone present appreciates the use of humor to voice their own feelings.

JOKERS AND GENDER

Jokers are often male. This isn't because women have less sense of humor than men. But playing the joker involves elements of leadership, domination, aggression, showmanship and risk-taking that males in contemporary society are socialized to more than females. Associated with this is a difference between the sexes in humor styles: women's humor is quieter than men's, private rather than public, interpersonally rather than organizationally oriented, and supportive rather than jokingly abusive. 'Taking the piss' is done much more by men than by women. So, overall, women practice and enjoy humor at work as much as men, but they do it as personal interaction rather than as the public performance that is essential to the central 'joker' role.

Here's a rare example of a female joker:

Savannah

'For fuck's sake …'.

The swear word sounds loudly over the normal quiet chatter of conversation in the open-plan office. Heads turn, and there are little gasps of surprise. It's a traditional insurance company with a largely polite, careful staff. That's not the kind of language they are used to, nor is it one that management wants to encourage. Who is the culprit? As they identify her, their expressions soften. It's only Savannah. And Savannah is special. Her direct manager, who has heard what she said, admonishes her, but in a gentle way. Savannah smiles apologetically and agrees that the criticism was 'fair enough'. Everyone understands that her head-turning 'for fuck's sake …', uttered in a moment of minor frustration, did not indicate aggression, but was more just an expression of her natural exuberance.

Savannah is in her mid-20s. Everyone agrees that she is the workplace joker. Her dark hair is cut short, framing an expressive face with clear blue eyes and a wide grin. Neither tall nor short, Savannah exudes a presence that seems to draw others toward her. She loves laughing, laughs a lot and really loudly, bursting into gales of giggles on the slightest provocation. Her colleagues enjoy her laughter so much that they tell her jokes just to hear her hearty mirth. But more often it is Savannah who creates the jokes and teases her colleagues in quick-witted exchanges of banter. In a 'mobile joker' routine, she will whirl around on her wheeled office chair, visiting friends, sharing a joke, laughing heartily, then moving on.

If she trusts you, Savannah will admit quietly that she doesn't like her job, specifically her main work task of cold-calling people about insurance. But she sticks with it and does it reasonably well. She loves her team and the company, and is willing to stay on and work toward a different role. The thing she likes most about the company is that it formally proclaims 'fun' as one of four key company values. 'Way to go!' thinks Savannah. She takes it literally and uses her natural good humor to intersperse the long periods of relative tedium with bouts of real fun.

Despite her apparent noisiness, Savannah is quieter and less risky with her joking than most male jokers. She is likeable and funny, and her vivacity, energy and fun sparkle, enhancing everyone's work day.

There are a few things to note about Savannah's role in this insurance company: First, Savannah's successful combination of male 'showing-off' and female 'sharing with a friend' styles of humor. Second, the good fit of Savannah's style with the 'have fun, but within certain cultural limits' ethos of the organization. Third, the fact that as the joker, Savannah enjoys significantly more popularity than most workers. Finally, we note that Savannah gets away with 'crossing the line' in her humor, as is evidenced in the mild disciplining that follows her profanity. This extra leeway applies to most workplace jokers but of course there are still limits that even they cannot transcend.

Why Jokers Do It

Why do jokers do it? Like all of us, jokers do what they do primarily as an expression of self. The humor motives of aggression, tension release, sexuality and sociability that we described in Chap. 2 apply especially to jokers. Their special traits of extroversion, exhibitionism, quick-wittedness and risk-taking fuel their words and actions. Most likely their practice of humor has been developed in previous settings, and has been reinforced by approval and laughter from previous colleagues. Even jokers who aren't very funny have their own inner dynamics driving their behavior. So whatever effect they may have on others, we should not forget that doing what they do almost certainly performs a useful function for them.

One joker told us, disarmingly, 'I want everyone to like me'. Often it's as simple as that: jokers like popularity. Some jokers have a 'joker' personality, and play the clown at home, in family and at leisure, making the joker role at work a natural extension of their character. Some simply enjoy giving pleasure to others, particularly making them laugh. Some, such as Boris the improvisational actor (Chap. 4) have a talent as a clown, mimic, improviser, stand-up comic or even singer or conjurer that they enjoy practicing in the workplace.

Others may have more complex or nefarious motives. The wish to be the center of attention may be an expression of a desperate, neurotic need to be loved. As we noted in Chap. 2, much humor is rooted in aggression. A smart joker may use humor to attack those he or she despises, or may channel the aggression of others against some real or imagined common enemy. We look at such aggressive humor in more detail in Chap. 9.

What Jokers Contribute

Entertainment

For most workers, the workaday world has its times—often long periods—of being tedious and boring. While one can relieve the tedium by keeping a magazine in one's desk drawer, or playing patience or checking out YouTube's latest sensations online, or having a chat with others round the water cooler, there is something special about live entertainment, and jokers such as Mac and Savannah are natural entertainers who love the limelight and can conjure up a feeling of theater in a trice.

Jokers deliberately take on the task of cheering others up. And each does so by channeling his or her natural self-expression into a format suitable for the special characteristics of their workplace. Their entertainment may be pre-planned, semi-planned or totally spontaneous. They create running or repeated gags that others find irresistible. They can defuse a tense or angry mood with a single quip. Sometimes they can make even one-to-one interactions seem funny and special. A skilled and sensitive joker is an asset to any workplace.

Morale

Jokers who are good at the role can 'add value' to their companies in terms of the good feeling, fellowship and morale that they create. This of course would never feature in a job description—'the employee is expected to contribute to organizational morale by generating laughter among colleagues at least five times per day'—nor in an annual performance evaluation.

Workplace humor is too incongruous, too intangible, too improvised, for the squared-off world of formal human resource management. Natural jokers such as Mac and Savannah are not selected, trained and timetabled but emerge spontaneously when their personal characteristics are placed in an environment where they can thrive. Having a good joker is therefore not something to plan for, but something to welcome and nurture as it emerges. But we must not forget that, as shown elsewhere in this book, that there are also 'bad jokers' around, natural comics who are, however, insensitive to the constraints of the organization's culture or the sensitivities of their coworkers, and do more harm than good.

Jokers, Influence and Power

Are jokers merely organizational ornaments, or do they have real power? The latter outcome, we suggest, is quite common: jokers are often more than a feel-good sideshow for other employees. Their special position enables them, like the court jesters of old, to use humor to challenge managers and managerial directives, and even to influence organizational policy and practice.

The Moving Target

It's the AlphaTech sales meeting, and as in the case of Clearview Products meeting mentioned above, it is not a happy occasion. The CEO has attended the meeting and is 'grilling' each salesperson in turn about their forecast sales versus actual sales. Most have failed to reach their forecasts, and they work hard to justify the discrepancy to the CEO. It comes to the turn of Zac, the recognized joker in the group, who, subjected to the CEO's searching questions of why he hasn't met the forecast, first tries to justify himself as the others have done, and then, pressed further, changes the tone by quipping, 'Oh well, I'll revise next month's forecast to zero sales'. His colleagues laugh loudly, and even the CEO smiles and moves on to another topic.

But the salespeople are all thinking the same two things. *Only Zac could have got away with that!* And *Zac has a point. We agree with him. Why can't the company see it?*

What is going on in this meeting? Here, we see two aspects of the joker's special position in the organization: *privilege* and *influence*. Zac is *privileged* in that he can make a joke about his own failure to achieve the forecast, and do so with impunity. The CEO laughs with Zac, where the same remark from any other salesperson would have infuriated him. But then, none of the others would have dared to say what Zac said. Zac has used his special role to deflect criticism.

Zac's *influence* as joker in this case is both actual and potential influence. His direct influence is immediate: his joke lightens the mood and induces the CEO to change the subject, thus saving not only Zac but also his colleagues from further criticism. In terms of potential further influence, there is an implicit challenge in Zac's comment: he is indirectly questioning the validity of the entire company forecasting system—a sore point not only to him but also, as he knows, to his colleagues. He is suggesting that if management presses the salespeople too hard then they can always respond by 'gaming' the system and forecasting low sales. While there is no evidence that the CEO notices the point that Zac is making, the fact that only he of all the staff could make it shows that organizational jokers have potential special influence. Eventually, messages like this from the joker may get through.

> **If We Feel Like It**
> In the Bytes company, a manager earnestly pleads with Mac's team to put in unpaid overtime to expedite an urgent order. When he has finished his request, there is a brief pause. Then Mac (the first joker highlighted in this chapter) says languidly:
> 'I suppose we *might* do it … *if* we feel like it'. He relaxes in his chair. There is a brief pause. The manager looks surprised. There is general laughter.

The manager is initially startled by the possibility of non-compliance with his request. Then he realizes it is a joke: there is no question of Mac and his colleagues not doing what he asks. Yet at the same time, Mac is able to convey an unspoken message, even a threat: perhaps 'Ok, but don't push us too far'. Again, only Mac, as the joker, could make such a comment. The manager reflects uneasily that behind Mac's relaxed demeanor and reassuring smile may lurk a hidden tiger.

Such jokes potentially remind managers of their subordinates' underlying wish to be treated with consideration, to be consulted, and to have some autonomy in their work. The joker's special privilege of being allowed to say the unsayable can therefore act as an effective conduit to the underlying feelings of rank-and-file workers, and help to mitigate any unthinking overenthusiasm by managers. Jokers are worth listening to, for their underlying messages as well as their jokes. After all, the court jester's role was to amuse but also to balance the 'hubris' of the king. Our corporate jokers similarly remind managers not to become too pompous or self-important—a useful function!

Pitfalls for Jokers

Despite the general centrality, approval and popularity of jokers, there are, however, some drawbacks and risks that jokers face. If you would like to be a joker, before you commit yourself fully to the role, you should think long and hard about these. Do the advantages of being the joker outweigh the disadvantages?

Unfortunately, some would-be jokers are simply very bad at it.

Competence

You may think yourself very funny, but others, for all sorts of reasons, may disagree. One potentially disconcerting response to humor is what one researcher called 'unlaughter'— deliberately not laughing, and putting on a neutral or even slightly disapproving expression in a situation which someone else considers to be funny or where others around you are laughing. You may find your best wisecracks are greeted with unlaughter. You may be poor at selecting your humor or at delivering it ('Sorry, I shouldn't have said that, that's the punch line'), or it may be out of line with the organization's culture (Chap. 3). Or maybe there is someone else who is simply a better joker than you are. If that is so, an alternative ploy may be to figure out whether there is a role for you in supporting or complementing his or her humor. But in most cases, it may be best to give up on the idea of being a joker, to keep a low profile, to join in humor appropriately as a group member and to consider alternative ways of achieving popularity or contributing to the organization.

Disruptiveness

In organizations, work has to get done. People have to communicate about work-related issues. Sometimes jokers just get in the way.

The Wise-Cracking Presenter
At Victory TV, Jeff is a presenter, a former chef and now a presenter and a judge in cookery shows. Jeff is bluff, extroverted, a little noisy and very popular with audiences. He's on his way to becoming a 'star' and is of course the best-paid worker in the show.

Jeff's a natural joker, wise-cracking his way incessantly through any conversation. This sometimes works quite well as a way of getting through to the interviewees he's dealing with in his shows. The trouble is, he doesn't know when to stop. And the TV crews he works with can't stand him, for a number of reasons. One is that they can't get anything done! They can't talk to each other or even hear each other across the babble of Jeff's incessant jokiness. Often while they're trying to prepare a scene, or the director is explaining the script to him, he will talk over them with his jokes. Second, many of his jokes are risqué and borderline offensive, and he seems to take pleasure in winding up the more politically correct. But of course, he's the 'talent' and they're the minions, so no one can tell him to shut up.

Revealingly, Jeff says, 'It's my way of keeping my energy up'. So— he's not doing it for the team: he's doing it for himself.

A joker doesn't have to be a joker all the time. Recognizing when, and with whom, it's appropriate to adopt the joker role, is a key joker skill.

Minority Disapproval

Believe it or not, however great the overall appreciation and enjoyment of a workplace joker, there are always likely to be some people around who have mixed feelings about the joker, barely tolerate the joker, or even hate the joker, or at least hate what the joker does. Jokers tend to be noisy and frequently distracting, and quiet workers or those who like to focus all their attention on what they are doing may find the constant humorous interruptions difficult to cope with. Others may simply be jealous of the popularity and attention that the joker enjoys. So while jokers are popular, they are not necessarily loved by all.

Non-promotability

We observe from our research that in every organization we have studied, senior managers are not jokers. The two roles seem incompatible. Perhaps managers are expected to behave with a degree of authority and dignity that is incompatible with the joker role. And, as we have seen, the normal joker's role is inherently subversive. Most likely the ranks of senior management include people who have in the past been workplace jokers: if so, they have changed their ways following promotion. Managers we have spoken to about this also tell us that the higher you go in the organization, the more serious would be the consequences if you used humor that others—even just one other—found demeaning or offensive.

G-string Fridays
Roger Sutton (real name) was the CEO of a large public company, but also the company joker. He constantly entertained his staff members through his idiosyncratic humor, much of it expressed to them through email. Some staff loved his approachability, laughter and off-beat, some would say outrageous, humor. But much of his humor was both sexual and sexist, such as his suggestion that women in the organization might like to be involved in 'visible G-string Fridays'. Was this, in the words of a male employee, 'innocent fun … goofing off and being flippant', or was it more serious? Although Sutton was apparently unaware that his material might be found offensive, a single female employee eventually laid a formal complaint, stating that Sutton's style of humor made her feel 'sick, exploited and vulnerable'. After the ensuing dispute proceedings and media attention, Sutton was forced to resign, stating that 'in future I will tell fewer jokes and no inappropriate jokes'.

In this case, as much as Mr. Sutton's humor, it was his power and authority, and his consequent high organizational and media profile that got him into trouble. Had he been a low-level employee, either no one would have noticed, or a warning from his supervisor would have induced him to change his style and avoid losing his job. In cases where humor is risqué, it is worth all potential jokers noting that the higher you are, the greater your likely fall.

In one of our research studies, we asked both managers and subordinates about their attitudes to humor used by managers. We got some mixed messages, and people were aware of the ambiguity of their responses. Overall, most of our workplace respondents agreed that while it was enjoyable for managers to use humor it was also risky, and that managers were not *expected* to be funny. Here are some of their thoughts:

'If my manager used humor, it would loosen him up and make me feel more at ease and allow me to see the real person.'

'Managers' humor can be misinterpreted as a personal attack, they are expected to drive the business—not to be funny…people don't expect them to be funny.'

'Humor used by managers is good as long as it is not overdone and as long as it does not obscure their position or point.'

The managers in question agreed: they all stated that they were cautious in using humor as if it was misguided or misplaced they might offend their subordinates. Here are some of our managers' thoughts about their own humor use:

'I have learned to be careful with humor as it can be an affront to my staff, can hurt feelings and damage my standing if it is inappropriate' (CEO).

'I make a joke about myself when it's obvious to others that I have stuffed up' (Sales Manager).

Overall, these managers felt that too much humor could damage their status and authority. They were even more cautious with newer employees. They admitted that they deliberately stuck to safe topics and self-deprecating humor.

Potential Misuse of Power

The dangers of mixing the 'joker' role with authority and power are even more evident in the case of Jake, the owner/CEO/joker of the IT company Adare (Chap. 3 and elsewhere). Described by some of his employees as 'the industry's biggest joker', Jake was renowned for his outrageous, violent, obscene, sexual and scatological humor, in which he constantly 'upped the ante' with pranks that became ever more outrageous. While many employees enjoyed working in such a 'way-out' culture, we have little doubt that his use of humor was as an overt form of control, and a minority of employees, particularly those who were singled out for mockery, resented it intensely but could do nothing about it. (As a footnote to any readers concerned at the apparent success of such an anarchic and (to some) offensive organization, Adare was later sold, the new owner changed its name, and all of the outrageous graffiti, posters and other signs of the antics of Jake and his colleagues were eradicated).

In the past, when the king joked, everyone laughed; but in today's subtler climate of human and employee rights, those in authority have to be a lot more careful about what they say. People such as CEOs, Board members and senior managers therefore have to be more careful than anyone else in their use of humor.

Takeaways
This chapter has two sets of takeaways. Firstly, we offer some guidelines to jokers on navigating this self-imposed role. Secondly, we provide some takeaways for managers on how to manage jokers and their activities.

Takeaway set 1: Jokers take note

- First of all, are you sure you are the right person to be the joker? You may think you are funny, but do others laugh, and if they do, do they mean it? Try to consider honestly whether the joker role is a good one for you.
- Is your humor planned or spontaneous? There's nothing wrong with a little planning ahead, but a joker needs to be able also to respond spontaneously in a humorous manner to day-to-day events at work. The story of 'Barry the singing sock' (Chap. 2) is a nice instance of an ongoing humor character planned in advance but able to draw laughter from time to time in response to the specific situation.
- If you know that you are the joker or one of the jokers in your workplace, enjoy your role, but, make sure that you know and understand your own work context, its professional norms and standards and where the boundaries lie for humor.
- Get to know your colleagues. Understand their sensitivities so that you know the 'no go' areas for humor. Pay attention to the responses of others to your humor, including ignoring it, 'unlaughter', negative facial expressions and verbal protests.
- Try not to exclude anyone from your joking but at the same time do not always pick the same person to joke with as they may feel picked upon.
- Although a joke may brighten up a stressful day, be aware of the times when there should not be any joking at all. Respect these times and don't be tempted to make jokes in these really tough times. For example, when someone has been 'let go', don't joke to cheer them up. If, however, they make a joke about the situation then it's ok to respond—but keep it gentle.

- Be aware of the impact of the joker role on your own personal image or brand. While it can be great to have social popularity through your clever humor, being seen as a 'joker' may preclude you from being taken seriously and considered for greater responsibilities. At times you may need to dial it back.
- Try to share the role of joker. It's good to have an 'offsider' or someone else that leads the joking when you need a break, don't feel up to it, or need to focus more seriously on your work tasks. Don't get competitive with other jokers as this is when joking can get out of hand and transgress workplace protocols.
- When you get it wrong, and it is likely that you will at some stage, apologize immediately, unreservedly and authentically to all those you have offended. Discuss with your manager if necessary. Don't hide your gaffe behind more humor. Take it quietly for a while.

Takeaway set 2: How to manage your joker

- Find out who is considered to be the joker(s) in your team, department and organization.
- Remember that your workplace joker fulfills an important role. Even if they annoy or overstep the mark at times, the light relief and pleasure they bring to working day is valuable. Treasure their input and tell them they are valued.
- Even clever, socially adept jokers may 'cross the line' sometimes and upset someone with their humor. A quiet, private warning may be necessary but combine this with recognition of their positive humor contributions. Make it clear if there are topics or forms of humor that are 'off limits'.
- Jokers are often socially popular, know everyone and are appreciated by their colleagues. Involve them in planning social or fun events as they may have some fresh ideas and be in touch with their colleagues' preferences.
- If it is necessary to develop workplace policies around humor, get the joker(s) involved in creating these. If they help to establish the boundaries, they may be more inclined to help maintain them. Also they will probably understand the limits for humor in their own work context.

CHAPTER 8

The Bright Side of Humor

The Laugh and Joke Song

Are things going wrong in your life?
Did you have a bad day at the office?
Did the manager shout?
Did the tea-lady pout?
Did your clients all call you a novice?

If these things are all true
I've a tip here for you,
And I want you to take it to heart.
If everything's bad,
And they're driving you mad …
Here's a new way of life you can sta-a-a-art ….

When things are getting to you and you think they can't get worse,
Just smile and sing and dance and laugh and joke!
Don't let them get you down, don't cry or whine or shout or curse,
Just laugh and watch your woes go up in smoke!
For there's something in the rumor that a smiley sense of humor,
Can put a silver lining on each cloud,
And the tea-lady and boss will very soon stop being cross,
But will fill your place of work with laughter loud!

© The Author(s) 2019
B. Plester, K. Inkson, *Laugh out Loud: A User's Guide to Workplace Humor*, https://doi.org/10.1007/978-981-13-0283-1_8

So if you're feeling blue, and get it right you cannot do,
And life's a great big heap of steaming shit,
The thing that you must do is just to laugh your way right through,
And shovel it away into life's pit!
'Cos it's very often said that we will very soon be dead,
Turn up our toes and make that deathly croak,
But until that final time, we can make the whole world shine,
If we smile and sing and dance and laugh and joke!
(One more time ...)

YES, SMILE AND SING AND DANCE AND LAUGH AND JOKE!

Recognize the song? Probably not. We were too mean to pay the royalties for songs of this type such as 'Bring me sunshine', 'Give a little whistle', and 'Always look on the bright side of life'. So we wrote it ourselves. Check such songs out; there are many of them out there in the media, and they all carry the same message, a message which is VERY popular: that humor is part of a package of positive traits centered on the concept of optimism that makes life's experiences more pleasant, and enables all difficulties to be overcome.

Is this true? As one might expect the answer is framed by such terms as 'partly', 'sometimes' and 'it depends'. In this chapter, we look at the 'bright side' of humor, which tends to validate these ideas, showing workplace humor to have huge beneficial effects on job satisfaction, morale, teamwork and often productivity. In the next chapter, we consider the 'dark side', which emphasizes how the wrong kind of humor can make things worse rather than better, causing offense, humiliation, conflict and loss.

THE PURPOSES OF HUMOR

First, however, we note that an important determinant of whether humor is positive or negative is its *purpose*. In everyday life and at work, humor is initiated with a variety of purposes Most importantly, it is a form of communication that is important in social interactions. Many humor studies focus primarily on these purposes.

Some people regard humor as a sort of 'tool' that can be used to improve social relations at work and make managers more likeable. Younger workers especially expect work to be enjoyable and to provide an element of fun. Our research has confirmed that most people, but not all, want humor to be part of their working lives. The 'managed fun' phenomenon that we documented in Chap. 5 is an example of humor being used deliberately to secure employee goodwill and commitment.

It is often assumed by the cheerleaders for workplace humor that such humor can only have positive purposes. A little surprisingly perhaps, this turns out not to be the case.

In an early research study, we observed many hours of working activity in several organizations, and interviewed many staff members about their own use and observation of humor at work. From these sources, we were able to draw up a list of the various possible purposes that workplace humor can be directed to. These are shown in the table below. From this we note that humor is multifaceted and so can have more than one purpose, indeed there can even be several operating simultaneously. We did warn you that humor is complicated!

---

1. 'Take the piss' or tease someone, for example banter
2. Break the ice, for example when colleagues or team mates don't know each other well
3. Foster camaraderie
4. Create rapport
5. Build relationships, for example in-groups
6. Show kindness, for example gentle inclusive joking, mild banter
7. Demonstrate inclusion, for example in-jokes, team acceptance
8. Break up boredom
9. Take a break from work tasks, for example have fun, play, joke, throw a squishy object
10. Help persuade someone, for example complimentary joking
11. Cope with stress and pressure, for example laughing at mistakes or difficulties
12. Display one's identity / personality, for example joker
13. Show off the culture (organizational or team), for example the fun-loving marketing team
14. Hide performance issues or deflect criticism, for example laugh it off, divert attention with a joke
15. Hide embarrassment, for example nervous laugh, self-deprecating comment, or diverting quip
16. Resist managerial directives/requests
17. Express hostility or displeasure
18. Make a point or criticism, for example soften the blow with a light quip
19. Initiate new staff members, for example mild hazing, teasing
20. Test others' boundaries/tolerances/ attitudes, for example a query in a joke
21. Violate norms and propriety, for example shock, or the joke format shields the joker

---

Suppose we rearrange these 21 functions into three groups: those which are clearly positive, those which are clearly negative and those which may turn out to be both or neither.

Generally positive
1. Break the ice, for example when colleagues or team mates don't know each other well
2. Foster camaraderie
3. Create rapport
4. Build relationships, for example in-groups
5. Show kindness, for example gentle inclusive joking, mild banter
6. Demonstrate inclusion, for example in-jokes, team acceptance
7. Break up boredom

Generally negative
8. Resist managerial directives/requests
9. Express hostility or displeasure
10. Make a criticism
11. Violate norms and propriety, for example shock, or the joke format shields the joker

Could be either, depending on circumstances, or whose point of view
12. Initiate new staff members, for example mild hazing, teasing
13. 'Take the piss' or tease someone, for example banter
14. Take a break from work tasks, for example have fun, play, joke, horseplay
15. Help persuade someone, for example complimentary joking
16. Display one's identity/personality, for example joker
17. Cope with stress, for example laughing at own or others' mistakes or difficulties
18. Test others' boundaries/tolerances/ attitudes, for example a query in a joke
19. Show off the culture (organizational or team), for example the fun-loving marketing team
20. Hide performance issues or deflect criticism, for example laugh it off, divert attention with a joke
21. Hide embarrassment, for example nervous laugh, self-deprecating comment or diverting quip

---

Consider, for example, the purposes listed under 'could be either'. The ostensible purpose of hazing (Chap. 5) may be to assist newcomers' transition into the organization, but it's quite possible that there is underlying aggression involved too. 'Taking the piss' may be employed to show camaraderie or as a 'put-down'. Taking a break from work may sound as if pausing to recharge one's batteries is intended, but the underlying objective may be to avoid working for as long as possible. The purposes of humor are not always positive. And, as we have shown, even if the purposes are positive, the humor may misfire, and the actual effects may be negative. The hazing and banter may shock and humiliate those subjected to it, and an excessive humor break may be damaging to the organization.

THE BRIGHT SIDE

Let's start, however, by noting the many positives of workplace humor. And let's remember that as well as being useful for the organizations we work for, workplace humor is also useful for us, the workers and managers who initiate and enjoy that humor. A well-chosen piece of banter, directed *by* a joker, at a colleague (the target), in front of an audience of other employees (observers), may bring pleasure to all three: the joker and the colleague feel appreciated, the audience is entertained and the wittiness brings laughter. If the target person manages a clever riposte, or an audience member a witty interjection, the momentary pleasure is enhanced and extended.

Nor are the positive effects of humor confined to positive circumstances. The lyrics from the satirical Monty Python song 'Always look on the bright side', which is sung at a crucifixion scene, are ludicrous and amusing but do illustrate a valid point: that even in the direst circumstances, humor can alleviate some of the pain and anguish. There is usually some humor at funerals as mourners remember the deceased in their funnier moments. Famously Sigmund Freud used the example of a man walking to the gallows to be hanged on a sunny Monday who quipped, in a form of 'dark humor': 'well, this week is starting nicely!' Freud suggested that he showed courage and resistance to his fate, and that this was a form of taking back some control of the situation, a rebellion against life's traumas that may provide inner liberation. From this analysis we get the phrase 'gallows humor', used when someone makes a joke about death or other dire circumstances: gallows humor abounds in specific occupations such as police and ambulance work, offering relief from the situations of death and degradation to which workers are exposed.

Creating fun at work is linked to humor and laughter and is professed to offer companies some competitive advantages such as staff retention and stress reduction. Some studies even go so far to suggest that humor at work improves performance and productivity although this link is not firmly established. After all it's hard to calculate ROI from humor! What our research, including many interviews with employees from many organizations, has shown is that workers *perceive* that humor makes them more productive due to its momentary 'release' from stress and overload. So, to our research participants, humor offers a kind of mini break that refreshes them so that they can continue working efficiently.

The great value of a 'humor break' is that it is often spontaneous, adding to the pleasure and surprise, can occur right where people are standing, sitting and working, and does not take a large amount of productive time away from work—though we do add the caution that it can distract others who may have been industriously completing their tasks. Humor in the office can also break a period of boredom and dullness: again, the workers we studied saw this as reviving and reenergizing which they believed improved their working ability. Some of the workplaces we studied even had a sort of 'humor rhythm' as seen in this example, narrated by Barbara:

Humor Breaks
Barbara writes:

At the AlphaTech (IT) corporate office after lunch and in the midafternoon, I observed that the office became really quiet for a couple of hours. Sales staff were usually out on calls and office-bound people had settled to serious tasks on computers with just a few quiet phone calls to break the almost silent atmosphere. Some days it even felt like a library and, wanting to fit in, I too quietly tapped away on my keyboard like my erstwhile 'colleagues'.

By about three o'clock most days, it seemed that everyone had had enough of this quiet, serious work and one or two men (usually the jokers—see Chap. 7) would create a 'humor break'. One day, funloving Craig threw a squishy ball across the office, hitting a colleague and promoting a squawk and retaliatory throw as a tit-for-tat ball battle commenced. Soon most people were laughing, quipping, teasing and enjoying the activity.

On another day, Zac, the foremost joker, roared through the open-plan space on a micro scooter, shouting and laughing. The jocular abuse flew, and much hilarity ensued. After a while the fun and jokes subsided and everyone got back on with their work. I could almost set my watch by it, and I watched with great anticipation each day as the unofficial three o'clock 'humor break' played out. I don't even think these workers realized their pattern, but it seemed to have a beneficial effect as the camaraderie, pleasure and shared enjoyment lingered after the humor had dwindled.

POSITIVE ATTITUDE, EMOTIONS AND WORK ADVANTAGES

Humor is an essential part of being positive but at the same time allows some social unruliness that attracts attention. Humor is associated with psychological capital, resilience, hope, optimism and self-belief. A survey of CEOs found that 98% prefer to hire people with a good sense of humor, and increasingly organizations are trying to tap into the humor advantage to create workplace cultures that prioritize humor and fun, for example Zappos, Southwest Airlines and Ben & Jerry's.

It is widely believed that fun cultures both attract potential staff and help to retain current employees, though, as we saw with the law firm Kapack (Chap. 3), this can backfire if employees attracted by the prospect of fun, find that the reality is 'no fun'. Many modern corporations articulate 'fun' as a key company value, a phenomenon we found in our studied companies. One finance company we studied even assessed how well employees and managers met the company 'fun' value, and this was analyzed in annual performance reviews with employees offering examples when they had either created or participated in organizational fun. Fun was taken very seriously and so to succeed in this company one had to embrace the 'fun' aspect of company life. It was notable that this company spent time and effort creating events for staff that constituted fun, and we saw these in operation as described below:

Lightening Up
It was Friday and people were tired from a busy week, but there was still a gentle buzz seeping through the office. Something was being planned, and staff were unsure just what it was and all of the team managers had mysteriously disappeared.

A small commotion at the entranceway saw all of the missing managers reappear, and both men and women were wearing tutus and fairy wings over their corporate attire! Laughter filtered through the office, and the managers played up to the staff, dancing, prancing and cavorting in their fairy costumes. Even better, they were carrying trays of ice creams and sweets and continued their balletic performance while distributing these treats to all assembled.

The goodwill lasted throughout the remainder of the day, and staff members agreed that it had been fun and funny to see their managers prepared to perform foolishly. And the ice creams were very enjoyable on a warm work day.

This simple fun activity created laughter and positive feelings. Psychological research reinforces the positive relationship between humor and mood. Even more than the treats and amusing managerial performance was the acknowledgement that managers were willing to risk looking silly in order to create fun and laughter. The positive emotions from this small event seemed noteworthy, and during the research this activity was referred to repeatedly. Of course, as previously stated, this company actually assessed both managerial and employee performance in reference to all of their company values including 'fun' and so managers possibly felt compelled to participate fully even though they may have felt uncomfortable or demeaned. However, the resulting positive climate was apparent, and even if this was just another work task, contrived by HR, it ably illustrates the bright side of humor and fun and the resultant goodwill and harmony.

One of the advantages of workplace humor is that it can temporarily mitigate workplace hierarchy and soften working boundaries. As seen above, a shared joke (or funny performance in this case) momentarily wipes out differences between managers and subordinates as everyone laughs together. Successful humor can make managers seem more likeable and can enhance and build workplace relationships which can be highly useful for workplace teams. We are not suggesting that all managers need to don wings and tutus and caper around the office; but good-naturedly joining activities, or even creating the occasional fun event—without, as we have noted, seeking to compel employees to enjoy 'managed fun' (Chap. 5) or to become the organization's joker (Chap. 7)—may foster positive emotions about work and strengthen group dynamics.

Groups and Teams

In work teams, humor can be part of group solidarity and may encourage belonging because knowing the jokes makes you an insider and an obvious group member. Teams often share 'in-jokes', jokey nicknames, mini rituals around working practices or tea breaks, humor about their families and so on. Humor in groups can build trust and morale, reduce stress and may enhance creativity. Humor is associated with a positive attitude as in 'being in good humor' or 'having an obvious sense of humor': a positive attitude and good sense of humor are seen as desirable attributes in workgroup members.

Some studies have shown that leaders' humor can improve group performance; and humor is almost always a part of the team-building that helps break down hierarchical barriers and creates emotional bonds. Cohesive groups that share jokes may perform better. Although banter between work group members can seem rude and confronting it often strengthens relationships and defines in-groups and out-groups. To put it plainly, as Brenda (Chap. 3) found, when she disrespected the humor culture of the team she had just joined, she was immediately ostracized by the team: if you are not included in the teasing and joking, you are not fully accepted as a group member.

LAUGHTER

In this book, we use the word 'laugh' or 'laughter' over 250 times. Indeed 'laugh' is the first word of our title. In nearly all cases, the word denotes a response of those present to humorous events. Laughter has a good press: songs of the type with which we started this chapter invariably urge us to laugh. Laughter, it seems, is a good thing. But what *is* laughter?

Laughter is an often involuntary physical reaction involving the facial muscles, diaphragm, epiglottis and larynx and voice. When something happens that we find amusing, our natural reaction is to laugh. Genuine laughter is a reasonably reliable guide to a person's feelings of amusement, though it may also be a socially expected echo of others' laughter.

Sometimes, however, laughter is suppressed: we try to close the mouth and choke off the voice because the full force of our laughter might be inappropriate in the social situation we are in: for example, when the boss is making a serious speech, but we are distracted by the remains of his peanut butter sandwich on his chin. There's a wonderful scene in the film *Monty Python's Life of Brian* where upright Roman soldiers, required to stand rigidly to attention, twist their bodies and faces into impossible contortions in order to avoid laughing at their general, who has just announced his name as 'Biggus Dickus'.

Laughter is contagious. Often one person's laughter helps others to 'see the funny side' of the situation, or simply to laugh as a way of sharing the other's pleasure, as when members of an audience laugh at a comedian's joke even though they don't understand it: they see and hear others laughing, and want to join in. And laughter, particularly communal laughter by groups of people, at work and elsewhere, is normally a socially acceptable, even desirable, form of behavior. We like laughing. We like making others laugh. Genuinely laughing releases endorphins in the body, making it pleasurable. Laughter is clearly a major element in the bright side of humor.

In addition, laughing appears to have health benefits. It relaxes the body, boosts the immune system, improves blood flow, reduces stress and anger and even burns calories! Physiological studies explain that laughing is a muscular activity that releases endorphins and offers a type of aerobic workout.

So workplace humorists can take a bow: their efforts apparently have positive effects beyond the workplace, in the overall pleasure and health they apparently bring to those who observe them!

STRESS REDUCTION AND COPING

It is well established that work is a key element of stress in peoples' lives. There is discussion about the ability of humor to help cope with stress and difficult workplace conditions. One study detailed how humor helps sex workers to cope with their work, and it has been shown that humor is very important in extreme work conditions such as police or armed forces work. Most of our research participants eagerly confirmed that humor and the resulting laughter relieve stress at work or stressful situations. This physical reaction combined with the emotional aspects of humor such as mood enhancement and positive feelings can create relief from stress, highly welcome in workplace environments.

Humor may reframe a stressful situation as an amusing interaction or event, and this makes it feel less threatening and changes negative emotions such as anxiety and fear into more positive and manageable feelings. Therefore, humor can be a coping strategy that is highly useful in the workplace. The behavior of other people such as work colleagues who can be irritating, stupid or incompetent generates many negative emotions. Making jokes either with (or sometimes about) other people can mitigate feelings of distress and unease. Of course, some humor that achieves this purpose can do so at the expense of others' feelings: this must be managed carefully. We discuss that side of humor in Chap. 9.

Ultimately humor can provide a way for people to alter perspectives on a stressful workplace situation and see it with different eyes so that things may not seem so bad after a laugh with a colleague or two. As discussed by

Rod Martin in *The Psychology of Humor*, humor is a way of standing off and looking at problems through a different lens. This can relieve anxiety and even may allow people to laugh at themselves and their own reactions to adversity which can help maintain positive self-esteem. As also asserted by Rod Martin, we do warn that when using humor to cope with stress, sometimes the humor can become somewhat aggressive, cynical, hostile or cutting (even about the self) and that a positive response to adversity through humor can become negative if the humor is too harsh or targeted at an individual. We therefore advise you to try and keep humor constructive.

HUMOR AND ORGANIZATIONAL EFFECTIVENESS

What about the argument that humor is a waste of potentially valuable working time? Well, what working time? A recent UK survey suggests that workers spend, on average, less than three hours of the eight or nine hours available per day actually working. What are they doing with the rest of the time? According to the research, they are 'checking social media, reading news, discussing out-of-work activities with colleagues, making hot drinks, smoking, texting, eating, preparing food, calling friends and partners, searching for new jobs'. Humor isn't mentioned, but we're prepared to bet that many of the activities are accompanied by humor. So there seems to be plenty of time for humor. The authors of the report suggest moving workers to a 20-hour week and ensuring that they work in a more concentrated way. That wouldn't leave much time for humor, but under present circumstances, there seems plenty of time for employees to experience it and to benefit from its positive effects.

Humor may provide pleasure and increased job satisfaction to employees, but does it make organizations more productive or successful? Although there is not a huge amount of workplace humor research, it is well recognized and acknowledged that humor is one of the ingredients for successful workplace functioning. But if there is a relationship between organizational effectiveness and humor, the causal direction may go both ways. Most likely humor is a cultural phenomenon, with the humor culture being a kind of by-product of the overall organization culture (Chap. 3).

THE DOWNSIDE OF THE BRIGHT SIDE

There are, however, limitations to the optimistic outlook.

Eternal Optimist

At our place, Charlie is the bright spark. He always has a smile on his face, always seems to be enjoying life. He's an eternal optimist; nothing ever gets him down. If things are going well for the company, there's no stopping him. Swinging around the place, laughing, joking, congratulating this one and that one, buying everyone a drink after work. And if things are going badly, he always finds a silver lining. Get a migraine, lose a customer, lose your job, get swindled by our rapacious management and Charlie will sit down with you in the tea room and help you to look for the positives. 'There's always a next time', he will say. Or 'You've still got your health, and that's the main thing'. And sometimes, 'I know what'll cheer you up. Have you heard the one about the …?'

Some people like that. Probably those who don't have enough to do. Personally, I hate it. He's so noisy. All that bonhomie drives me crazy. It's so hard to concentrate when he's doing his thing. I can never get anything done.

There are rumors about layoffs. Could be Charlie. That might wipe the smile off his face.

Charlie is a living example of one of the key limitations of the bright side of humor. You can take it too far. Your intentions may be good, but your humor can get in other people's way. Sometimes, too, optimism and joking are hiding from reality and thereby becoming unable to deal with it. Sometimes you need to face reality without the protection (and distortion) of humor.

'POLLYANNA'

Google 'workplace humor' and you will find many websites brimming with good news. They teem with jokes, cartoons, posters, games, pranks and other humor paraphernalia that they insist will have everyone in your workplace cracking up with laughter. And indeed, *some* of what they

suggest may well have just that effect on *some* of the people in their organization. But there will be others who can't stand even the thought of
what they would call 'forced' or 'artificial' humor of this type (see 'managed fun', Chap. 5). And many of them may say that overdoing workplace
humor is an example of '*Pollyanna-ism*'. We agree. So what or who, is
Pollyanna?

In the 1913 novel *Pollyanna* by Eleanor H Parker, the title character,
Pollyanna Whittier, has a philosophy of life based on the positive: Pollyanna
believes one can always find something to be happy about, even in the
most difficult circumstances. Poor people can be glad they are not sick,
sick people that they are not poor, and poor, sick people that the weather
is good. 'Pollyanna-ism' means having unshakeable optimism even when
confronting the most adverse circumstances. And optimism and positive
thinking are invariably recommended as including, retaining and using
one's sense of humor as a means of coping. The Pollyanna phenomenon
can be summed up in the song with which we opened this chapter, and in
the advice of Lord Baden-Powell, the founder of the Boy Scouts: 'A scout
smiles and whistles in all circumstances'. Optimism, willingness to 'smile
and whistle' and retaining one's sense of humor are lauded by management gurus on the web, and in books such as Norman Vincent Peale's
classic *The Power of Positive Thinking*.

While on the face of it Pollyanna-ism is an appealing philosophy, many
would criticize it as being naïve. There is, however, another side to the
'good news' story of optimism at work. In the novel, Pollyanna's faith in
her belief in the positive is tested when she loses the use of her legs in an
accident. In contemporary usage, the term 'Pollyanna' has begun to
assume negative rather than positive qualities. It often refers to someone
whose optimism is excessive to the point of naivety, or who is unrealisti-
cally unable to accept the facts of a bad situation and to respond appropriately. People who 'smile and whistle' as their home burns down around
them or their competitor wipes out their company with a superior product
are not necessarily behaving in a way that is good for them.

We are also reminded of the 'false consciousness' conundrum. In the
early and mid twentieth century, 'human relations' became a popular
approach to management. Managers were encouraged to cultivate warm,
positive relationships with staff and to permit on-the-job socializing,
including humor, as a way to raise morale and thereby productivity. The
'false consciousness' came from the way in which the accentuation of the
positive could be used manipulatively to draw workers' attention away

from the poor pay, insecure employment, unhealthy conditions and so on, which in many cases characterized their jobs.

Concluding Comments

So there we have it. Workplace humor, benignly and sensitively practiced within an overall culture that supports it, is a potential boon to nearly all, if not all, workplaces. It benefits both individuals and organizations. It can be deployed to the best of purposes. It boosts morale. It relieves stress and tension. It promotes laughter. It may even enhance individual health and organizational productivity.

But there is always a 'but'. As we have quietly noted throughout this chapter, if humor is done badly, it can go wrong—with catastrophic effects. And it is to those that we turn in the next Chap. 9.

Takeaways

- Managers need to help promote balance when encouraging humor at work. Balancing the right type of humor with the right amount can really benefit workers and managers.
- Managers need to note that enthusiastically endorsing humor and fun might not necessarily result in quantifiably better performance or productivity. However, encouraging humor and fun does make people *feel* that they are more productive and refreshed which is beneficial for most people. So encourage a lighthearted approach to work whenever possible.
- Constructive humor can offer a valuable stress relief for busy workers and managers. Managers need to aim for promoting forms of humor that are enjoyed by as many people as possible.
- Managers who can make fun of themselves in a humorous moment or a fun activity usually create goodwill within their team. Some good-natured fun at your own expense can humanize and soften a manager.
- Managers need to be aware of the overoptimistic, overenthusiastic humorist. While they may fulfill a useful role in the workplace, too much humor and fun can irritate others especially when it is naïve or becomes falsely positive. A gentle but kind word may be necessary to reduce this effect but should be coupled with recognition of the humorist's value and good intentions.

- Managers of humor should learn, if they can, the difficult practice of distinguishing between the different forms of laughter, because they convey different responses to the situation. If they spot 'unlaughter' in one or more people, it can be useful to check in with them and ensure that they are ok with the humor and/or fun.

CHAPTER 9

The Dark Side of Humor

The Immaculate Conception
At Victory TV, it is the first day of a new production, which is about
the countryside and headquartered on a farm. The production team
of 15 has been called to a meeting with the head of the production,
Gudrun, to discuss what they'd be doing. Gudrun has called in the
Victory health and safety officer to give a briefing on farm safety. The
officer goes over some basics, then begins to talk, for any staff who
might be pregnant, about some specific rules around pregnancy on
farms.

At this point Harper, a senior member of the team, arrives (late as
she's been held up in traffic) and takes her seat with the new team,
most of whom she doesn't know and several of whom will be report-
ing directly to her. The health and safety officer helpfully repeats that
she has just been explaining about being pregnant and working on a
farm.

At this point, Gudrun—the boss—lets out an enormous cackle.
'Pregnant!' she exclaims. 'Chance would be a fine thing. If that one
was pregnant it'd have to be an immaculate bloody conception! She
hasn't had sex since the Dark Ages!' Hugely amused by her own
joke, she laughs uproariously. Heads swivel to look at Harper, and

© The Author(s) 2019
B. Plester, K. Inkson, *Laugh out Loud: A User's Guide to Workplace
Humor*, https://doi.org/10.1007/978-981-13-0283-1_9

the rest of the group let out a few nervous titters, but no one seems very sure how to react. Harper quickly apologizes for being late and, to move things on, asks the health and safety officer an unrelated question.

But inside she feels humiliated. She is furious. 'I'll never work for that woman again', she tells her friends afterwards.

In this incident, what was Gudrun trying to do? Did she intend to humiliate her colleague, or did she simply assume that Harper would see the joke and laugh along with her? If we look back at our theories of humor (Chap. 2), it is likely that the sheer *incongruity* between the idea of pregnancy and the entrance of a colleague that Gudrun knew was living a chaste life struck her as funny, and her extroverted personality took over to present the joke without thought of possible negative effects. But perhaps, too, her inner wish to demonstrate *superiority* over the others present, including Harper, was the driving force behind her remarks. Perhaps she even intended to hurt. Either way, her remark was damaging. Humor can wound. Humor can even kill. We have to be careful with humor. In this chapter, we look at humor's 'dark side'.

As we have indicated previously, humor has a good press: it is currently presented, particularly, on the Internet, as a 'good thing'. In this chapter, we work to redress the balance and indicate something of the 'dark side' of humor: the deep distress it can both signal and cause; bitter humor, the expression not of fun but of desperation; inner disgust and revulsion at what a joker considers to be funny; and hurt at one's deepest personal feelings or identity being ridiculed.

In this book, we have already chronicled many instances where the effect of humor was principally 'dark' for its targets: the female ski instructor who was revolted by the sexual innuendo of her male colleagues' prank and left the organization (Chap. 1); the mother of a child with a disability who was upset by a joke about disability (Chap. 2); the female consultants who were deeply offended by their male clients' sexual jokes but felt they had to go along with them (Chap. 4); the warehouse worker terrified by being stranded at the top of a forklift by her coworkers (Chap. 4); and the workers who objected to their boss jocularly inviting them to 'G-string Fridays' (Chap. 6).

In each of these cases, the offended parties were female. We do not mean to imply that only women can be negatively affected by workplace humor, and we will, in this chapter, provide examples of men also suffering through misguided workplace humor. But there is little doubt that men and women overall have different standards and expectations when it comes to humor. We noted in Chap. 6 that female 'jokers' are few and far between, and that women's characteristic humor preferences are different from men's—less aggressive, less exhibitionist, more interpersonal.

We believe that much, if not most, harmful workplace humor is based on the *superiority* motivation we discussed in Chap. 2. Superiority-motivated humor typically involves explicit or implicit disparagement of another, or even *schadenfreude*, taking pleasure in the pain of others. In television programs such as *America's Funniest Home Videos*, for example, unwitting participants such as skateboarders are filmed being subjected, often through their own risk-taking and clumsiness, to terrible indignities and potentially bone-shattering accidents. Typically, the scene is quickly shut down (before we can find out whether the victim has been badly hurt), the studio audience roars with laughter, and we, at home watching it all on TV, are meant to do the same. Yes, some people *enjoy* being on television suffering humiliation, while others enjoy watching that humiliation. But at least targets and audience are unknown to each other, and the 'jokes' are presented as images rather than in reality.

But not everyone finds *America's Funniest Home Videos* funny: some people find them offensive and switch them off, or, more likely, don't switch them on. Workplace humor, unfortunately, is something you can't easily switch off. Typically, it is *there*, in front of you, much of the time when you are at work, and you have to put up with it, though, as we will show in Chap. 10, if you don't like it there are things you can do to prevent its recurrence.

To get a better handle on the kind of distress and dysfunction that workplace humor can cause, let's take another look at our old friend Adare the IT company.

Sensing the Dark Side
As you will recall from previous chapters, Adare's entire culture, largely created and sustained by a charismatic CEO, involved extreme humor. You will recall the endless laughter, pranking and vulgarity, the collapsing chairs, the farting cushions, the gay porn clock, the food fights and so on.

On the surface, far from such antics representing any 'dark side', staff members (who we interviewed in depth about their responses to humor) were happy with, and even proud of, their humor culture. They enjoyed being zany, 'anti-PC', and shocking to outsiders: and having 'no limits' on humor. Most contributed energetically to the atmosphere. We could see too that despite the humor breaks and distractions, the humor culture thus contributed to high-energy work practices, morale, pride in the organization and above-average performance.

But there was a downside to the story, perhaps an uneasiness that staff felt, a recognition that all-out humor can carry costs.

First of all, staff recognized that the humor at Adare was 'top down', that is, created and sustained by Jake, the owner/CEO, and therefore was potentially a tool for power. Jake reinforced this impression by providing—alone among the organizations we studied—no managerial restraint of humor. In fact, Adare enjoyed—or suffered— rather the opposite: managerial encouragement for the humor and pranks to become ever more outrageous, even to the point of inflicting emotional disturbance, embarrassment and even physical pain on employees. Adare was therefore a very 'macho' organization where even if you were upset by the humor you wouldn't show it, rather you would 'take it like a man' and 'give as good as you get', thus perpetuating and even magnifying the culture.

For example, Jake took advantage of the temporary absence of Ann, an office administrator, from her desk. He had another male employee take a photograph of his bare buttocks, then uploaded the photo to replace Ann's screensaver. Sexual harassment, surely? Ann didn't see it that way. When she returned and saw the image, she first screamed, then laughed and swore revenge on the jokers. Jake would say, 'No, just the way we do things round here. Everyone loves it, there's no harm in it. Ann understood it and enjoyed it, what business is it of anyone else?'

But then, Jake was not just an average joker, he was the CEO and owner of the business, with the power not just to 'set the tone', but to bully or fire the employees. Ann may have felt uneasy or even offended, but if so she showed it only momentarily. She knew how to play Jake's game and did so, laughing along with the others. Jake's behavior, insulated by his authority, was virtually risk free. But his apparent use of his power raises question marks.

Second, some staff members specifically described how staff members might be 'picked on', 'spit on' and 'exploited' in humor, which sounds close to modern definitions of workplace bullying. Others told us that they recognized the potential for harm, particularly to more sensitive individuals. Sometimes the humor had gone too far and people had been hurt, either physically or psychologically. They were aware that while some might take put-downs in their stride, others might be hurt, and that sometimes one had to 'back off' from using humor with a more sensitive staff member.

A number of the staff were Korean. A staff member told us, 'The Koreans are the butt of jokes and get the piss taken out of them—but they love it'. We weren't so sure. Because Korean culture is imbued with the values of Confucianism—modesty, respect for authority—the style of humor in Korea is likely to be very different from that in Western countries, and almost the antithesis of that at Adare. Weren't the Koreans shocked at Adare's antics? The Koreans seemed to enjoy the jokes—but how did they feel inside? Were they simply playing along to keep their lives simple, and avoiding confronting the 'dark side'?

We had particular concern for a staff member called Adrian. As another employee explained, 'Adrian .... is the butt of a lot of jokes, mainly because he comes across as being really innocent and unable to stand up for himself'. One can imagine that such a person might indeed feel alienated and distressed in a 'no-holds-barred' organization such as Adare, the more so when his very sensitivity made him a prime target for the aggressive masculine humor of his colleagues.

Lastly, we might mention the effect of Adare's humor culture on staff recruitment and turnover. This cut both ways. Some Adare staff had joined the company specifically because of its industry reputation as a fun place to work. Typically, such staff enjoyed the constant hilarity: it was what they had come for. And of course members of any organization who don't like the culture can always resign and go elsewhere (assuming there is somewhere else to go). This was very much Jake's attitude: 'If they don't like it they can leave'. But two employees resigned while we were there, both confiding to us that they found the humor distracting and embarrassing. Sadly, their impending departure, on one month's notice, only caused them further mockery and embarrassment.

In Adare, in perhaps in a more concentrated form than in most organizations, we begin to see the dark side of humor. The zany, noisy, vulgar, scatological atmosphere had made Adare not just a sociable fun park in which the staff could feel at ease and give of their best (and for some it was just that), but also, potentially and sometimes actually, a shooting gallery where everyone had a license to kill, and the sensitive were the prey.

Fortunately, the staff were mostly smart and virtuous enough to recognize the immorality of teasing, offending or denigrating (even if it was a joke) to the point of distress. They therefore exercised sufficient self-control in most cases. Nevertheless, the collective nature of humor cultures makes them potentially dangerous. Had Adare not been wound up, we fear that much greater harm might eventually have been done.

Most organizations are not like Adare. But most organizations have their share of employees who, underneath their pleasant exteriors, are wrestling with personal demons relating to superiority or aggression or sex or race, and who find that the social sanctioning of humor that most workplaces practice provides them with just the right venue to express their frustrations.

Can't Take a Joke
Dylan returns to his desk and sits down. His colleague Tom, nearby, initiates a conversation.

'You've been away from your desk for a while.'

'Just a few minutes.'

'So—where were you?'

'I went to the toilet, if you must know.'

'Oh, the toilet, eh?' (Tom gives a knowing leer). 'And what were you up to in there?'

'What do you think? The usual. Anyway, it's none of your business.'

'Oh, *touchy*! You were away a long time. There must be more to it than that.'

'Look, leave me alone. I want to get on with my work.'

'I bet you had a girl in there.'

'What? Why, you—'

'Oh-oh! You're blushing! Hey, look, guys. Dylan's blushing!'

Two of Tom's friends, who have been eavesdropping the conversation, look round. 'So he is!'. They all laugh.

'I am not—'

'All because I caught him in the toilet with a girl ....'

'You did not—'

'Or was it a *boy*? You see, guys, with Dylan you can never be too sure.'

General laughter. Dylan is close to tears. A manager hears the disturbance and intervenes, 'What's going on here? Dylan, are you ok?'

'Um, yes, I'm all right. Just a little hay fever.'

'And you, Tom. What's all this about?'

'Just having a little joke, Mr. Philips.'

'Well, just remember we need that job done by four. There's no time for jokes.' The manager moves away. Tom turns to Dylan with a fierce whisper.

'Now look what you've done! What is it with you, Mr. High-and-Mighty Dylan? Fucking *tears*, is that it? You're useless. Can't take a joke. Fucking pansy!'

It seems likely that this exchange was driven by Tom's internal aggression and desire to feel superior (see Chap. 2). Perhaps sexual frustration was another cause. Or he may have been showing off—trying to demonstrate superiority through exhibitionism—to his friends, whose connivance and laughter demonstrates the social dimension of humor and makes it the more humiliating for Dylan. Note, too, the habitual defense of the habitual offensive humorist—'just having a little joke, Mr. Philips'—and the connivance of the victim—'I'm all right, just a little hay fever'—who realizes that even worse is in store for him if he tells his boss the truth.

Sorry if we seem like spoilsports, but we consider that such 'humor'—if it can be called that—typically tells us more about the inadequacies of the joker than anything about the victim. It is a form of bullying, and is often associated with other, non-humorous, bullying behavior. It is mean spirited and usually totally undeserved. It can damage victims psychologically. It can cause damaging conflict for the organization and can even escalate into violence.

But what can be done about it? Jokers, victims and managers can all take remedial action, as we will show in Chap. 10.

HUMOR AND 'POLITICAL CORRECTNESS'

In recent years, the term 'political correctness' has gained much currency. Political correctness means the avoidance of words or actions that may exclude, marginalize or offend specific groups who are disadvantaged or discriminated against, principally but not exclusively women, gay people and non-white ethnic groups. While political correctness appears to have the praiseworthy intent of protecting the weak against the strong, it has, in the eyes of some, gradually acquired negative connotations of fussy, unnecessary interference with everyday language and action in order to provide unfair advantage or protection to such groups.

How much humor is politically incorrect, does that matter, and what can and should be done about it?

Punch Her in the Face
In the organization's staff kitchenette, where members come for coffee and snacks, there's a poster. A man stands with his back to the camera. His legs are apart and his right hand is coiled into a fist: an aggressive stance. Between his legs we see a woman, cowering on the floor, clearly distressed, frightened and crying, her hand apparently wiping blood from her injured face. The caption reads, 'PUNCH HER IN THE FACE ... TO PROVE YOU'RE RIGHT'.

The organization employs mainly men, though there are a few women. It was a male employee who put the poster up. No one has taken it down. On seeing it for the first time, a few of the men, and one or two male visitors, have laughed. Employees, male and female, say, 'It's just a joke'. A male employee explains that 'we don't go in there—the kitchen's only for women ... anyway the kitchen is just a pathway for beer'.

This story, about an almost certainly politically incorrect image, raises questions. Why, when most people are appalled by the implicit support in the poster for male domestic violence, do some men find it funny? Such men might say, well, it's the man who is put down. How could any man be so stupid as to think he had proved his argument correct by hitting a woman? Isn't the poster merely ironic? Women and some men would say that any display that tries to use such an image for a humorous effect, and that may have the effect of making such behavior seem normal, is outrageous and should be banned. If there is any humor there at all, it is completely eclipsed by the offensiveness of the accompanying image. And of course workplaces such as the one in which this open display of male domination is displayed, are contexts in which it is acknowledged that women are seriously disadvantaged. As we said early in this book, humor is contentious.

In Chap. 2 we noted that humor is driven by the needs and drives of the humorist. While some of these motives, such as sociability, appear benign, others, particularly the desire for superiority—which may include the desire to seem or to be superior to those of a different gender or racial group—and the release of sexual or aggressive tension, are more problematic. What was the psychology driving the artist who created the punch-her-in-the-face image, the organization that acquired and marketed it, the employee who posted it and those who laughed at it?

One suggestion is that they may be driven by a male superiority/aggression fantasy and moreover assume that others, sharing the fantasy, will likewise be able to share the joke. Another is that the growing public distaste for open displays of male superiority and aggression drives such feelings into darker, subtler corners of human experience, such as humor. In organizations like Adare, a masculine culture dominates, to which male and female employees must conform, and in which humor is a major form of expression: the humor at Adare was masculine, homophobic, sexist and obscene, and we were able to observe there changes in at least one female employee as a result.

Humor and Organizational Resistance

Putting It to the Committee

Employee: 'Did the Executive Steering Committee approve my project?'
Boss: 'We agreed a pre-decisional draft framework for making the decision.'
Employee: 'Does that mean anything?'
Boss: 'It depends what you mean by *anything*.'

No, not a true story, but a fine invention by the cartoonist Scott Adams, whose 'Dilbert' comic strip lampooning the absurdities of modern organizations has been delighting us for decades. Every institution and every individual is in some way absurd, and much humor arises from recognizing these absurdities, pointing them out, and enjoying them. And, as Adams has made his reputation and his living out of realizing, the business organizations of the late twentieth and early twenty-first centuries, are all, in their way, ridiculous (as well as frequently being worthwhile and high performing and good places to work in).

It's not surprising, therefore, that much workplace humor is gently or aggressively directed against the organizations we work in and in particular their managers and other authority figures. The Humor Climate Questionnaire we introduced in Chap. 3 has a dimension called 'Outgroup Humor'—humor that is directed outside the group at another target, in this case higher-level management. In essence, out-group humor may be a form of either mild or substantial *resistance* against the status quo. But how does this work, and what, if anything, should managers do about it?

In joining the organization, we surrender ourselves to a *structure* of job descriptions, authority relationships, rules and regulations; and a *culture* of norms, dress codes, taboos and the like (see Chap. 3), all of which in some way constrain our freedom and all of which have their own oddities. We gasp at the incompetence of some of our colleagues, at the antics of autocratic or self-absorbed bosses, at stupid rules, at the bureaucratic breakdowns, and at the nonsensical manager-speak:

The Corporate Bullshit Generator

'Our cutting-edge brandings diligently enforce flow chartings, providing value-adding opportunity and global reach .... Our methodology will boost the coordinated, fine-grained and radical time-to-value, and we will work together to champion our scalabilities to achieve an incremental profits growth .... Hyperaware synergies turbocharge movable and curated value chains .... Internally and externally, the mediators conservatively incentivize a synchronized criticality .... The established targets expediently prioritize a goal-oriented social sphere .... Collaboration and action items gradually deepen our time-phased and/or convergent recalibrations .... etc. .... etc. ..... etc. ....'

When we look at such a pastiche of sloganeering, it is not hard to see why the situation in which we find ourselves, if it does not generate anxiety, misery and anger, should at least generate humor: the triggers of absurdity, tension release, aggression and sociability (Chap. 2) are all likely to be involved. The humor may be directed against the general institution of working life, or against the specific organization in which we are employed, or both. And, because many of us are insufficiently creative to express our feelings in a directly 'funny' way, an entire industry has sprung up to help us, Scott Adams' Dilbert being just one example.

Researcher Martin Parker has studied the humor 'artefacts' that we assiduously acquire to express our feelings. Here's an example of a humor artefact, from our research:

> **Company Performance**
> This notice, printed from an Internet post, was pinned to the wall in the Bytes office:
>
> *Another month ends*
> *All targets met*
> *All systems working*
> *All customers satisfied*
> *All staff eager and enthusiastic*
> *All pigs fed and ready to fly*

This notice wryly lampoons company performance, with a mild sting in the final line. The gentle joke could transfer to most customer-based organizations.

Other examples include Dilbert or other anti-work or anti-organization cartoons taped to an office door or partition; coffee mugs with the motto, 'You don't have to be crazy to work here—but it helps'; photoshopped images of the company's 'top brass' with Hitler-like moustaches or distorted faces; 'Fuck work' badges and T-shirts; stamping tools with the motto 'I haven't time to read this CRAP!' Again, some of these symbols would be unacceptable in some organizations: the extent of their open display will depend on the culture of the organization.

Such displays—which may be paralleled by more specific comments and jokes in office chatter and gossip—may be regarded as forms of 'resistance' to the status quo—mute protests against the nine-to-five office life, or distant unreachable bosses, or organizational pretension. But frequently, they are not potentially damaging displays of underlying discontent and rebellion, but merely harmless rueful reminders that the world of work and of the particular organization is bound to be imperfect, and that recognizing such imperfection through humor helps to fill the working day more pleasantly. A comment such as 'you don't have to be crazy to work here—but it helps' may be a compliment to the organization rather than a criticism of it: most people like the idea of a little craziness in their workaday lives.

Much more troubling for management may be situations dominated by hostile 'us and them' emotions, where humor is used as a weapon to demonstrate employees' total cynicism or hostility about their work or about the organization, particularly their contempt for management. Here, humor can even become a tool used in the service of exacerbating conflict or even changing power relationships.

HUMOR AS SUBVERSION

In developed economies, the manufacturing assembly lines of old have largely been automated out of existence, but they have often been replaced by workplaces where service work is equally routinized and microregulated. In recent years, call centers handling customer enquiries and complaints have gained an unwanted reputation for such practices laying severe constraints on employees' autonomy, setting near-impossible targets, paying minimum wages and resisting all attempts by the workers to unionize. In addition, the work is naturally routine and repetitive, and stresses the call operators by requiring them, whatever the provocation, to remain courteous and helpful to customers. It's a recipe for poor labor relations.

Making Call Center Work Bearable
At the T call center, some of the humor was interpersonal—'taking the piss' as elsewhere. Mark, Shona and 'Norrie the Hun' were the jokers-in-chief (see Chap. 7), but everyone participated. Much of the humor, despite a huge banner declaring 'COMMITTED TO PUTTING THE CUSTOMERS' NEEDS FIRST', was at the

expense of the customers: for example, by pressing a 'mute' button on their telephones, staff members could mock, mimic and ridicule customers to entertain their colleagues without being heard by the customer, or, in breaks, run 'my customer is even worse than yours' competitions. These events took on a ritual quality, much like a modern version of 'Banana Time' (Chap. 5).

Some humor was, however, directed against management. For example, a photograph of 'The new office space' —a toilet with a computer, keyboard, printer and phone all placed within handy reach of the occupant— reinforced the message that 'work never stops'. A running gag was created when management appointed as the boss of a French-speaking team of agents, a manager who spoke no French! One agent, having said goodbye to a customer, continued, in French, in earshot of the manager, who understood nothing, 'Thank you very much for calling. We will send someone round to kill your wife and family', then reported in English to the manager how successful the call had been, while his colleagues struggled to contain their laughter.

A different situation existed at another call center, E, where the managerial regime was distinctly more repressive, with tight managerial control, tougher targets, closer surveillance of agents, a requirement to spend 97% of hours dealing with clients, a managerial antipathy to collective worker representation and a history of conflict.

At E, humor was of a different order to T. It was almost exclusively, and viciously, directed against the organization's managers, who were regarded as bumbling, self-serving, autocratic idiots. Managers were all subjected to anxiety-producing and humiliating taunts—but always in a way where the material was ambiguous, or was expressed collectively or anonymously rather than individually, so that nobody could be identified and disciplined. For example, when the dress code for the center was changed, and all the agents were required to wear a business shirt and tie, they collectively decided that they would adhere to the new rule, but would each wear a shirt and tie and other clothing that looked as bizarre and unprofessional as possible.

A group of workers were defined by management, and took pride in the description, as 'bad boys'. These agents were determined to establish a union presence in the organization, and their humor, was intended to combat their 'unjust' employer. They coopted negative humor into negotiating, for example deploying scathing, profane sarcasm and satire into the (anonymous) written demands: their humor was an absolute expression of aggression and hatred but also part of a deliberate strategy of seeking greater power in the organization.

Case studies adapted from Phil Taylor and Peter Bain (2003), 'Subterranean worksick blues: Humor as subversion in two call centres', *Organization Studies*, 24(9), 1487–1509.

The humor at these call centers ran the gamut from light relief from the tedium of work, through semi-angry tension release through mockery of managers and customers, to the aggressive use of humor in deliberate attempts to confuse and humiliate another disliked group. In addition, black humor was used as a (minor) tool in a struggle for greater organizational power, and also, we think, as a cry of desperation from a group of workers who found their situation intolerable.

Overall, the humor at T was a useful relief from boredom, a mild subversion of management, but directed more at tension release than at deliberate resistance. But the humor at E was of a different order. This was humor in the service of full-blooded resistance to work and organization in general, and to specific managerial groups in particular. Such humor, at its extreme, is a representation of sheer aggression (see Chap. 2), even hatred, and is also *collective,* the expression not just of a single individual but of an entire workforce. It may therefore be may be deeply hurtful and potentially damaging to those who endure it.

But in such cases, the humor is merely an outer manifestation of deep-seated organizational problems. It therefore cannot be 'managed' in the same manner as humor in the more collaborative organizations on which this book focuses: until the deeper-seated problems of the situation are resolved, the humor of the workers in these organizations will continue to be barbed and to have few boundaries. Management won't be able to fix it without changing their entire organization, and any attempt to do so is destined to fail.

CONCLUDING COMMENTS

In relation to both humor that offends and humor that expresses resistance, the dark side seems very much a matter of degree: from gentle ribbing to merciless taunting, from 'winding up' the other person a little, to subjecting them to bitter sarcasm. The dark side is potentially there in all organizations where humor is used, and that is basically all the organizations that exist. In some cases, such as Adare IT and the E Call Center, it may be so deeply ingrained as to make eradication impossible without massive radical action. We suspect that even Jake, the owner/CEO of Adare, could see that in his company he had inadvertently created and encouraged a dark monster that he could no longer control and that was ultimately unsustainable, and perhaps that is why he sold the organization.

In most organizations, however, the dark side, while always lurking as a potential destructive force, is normally minor, localized and manageable. The bright side (Chap. 8) can be enhanced, and the dark side minimized, by the conscious shifting, by all parties, of the humor boundaries we first mentioned in Chap. 3. In this endeavor, the organizational humor players we mentioned in Chap. 1 can all play a part: the jokers who lead humor; the 'targets' or 'victims' of humor; the observers and 'audience' who see and respond to humor; the gatekeepers, formal and informal, who police humor boundaries; and the managers who are responsible for the humor in all situations. These are dealt with in our final Chap. 10.

Takeaways

- Be aware that humor can hurt and offend people. Be alert to destructive humor in your team or organization. Dark or negative humor may have to be discussed, identified and discouraged. While it's not fun being the 'humor police', you may have to take on this responsibility to avoid workplace dissension.
- Humor can be sexual, sexist, racist and highly aggressive. Recognize the potential for so-called humor to perpetrate serious misdemeanors such as sexual or racial harassment and bullying. Such humor is unacceptable nowadays and must be firmly discouraged and dealt with.
- When you manage dark forms of humor, the fact that what is funny to one person may be unacceptable and offensive to another, makes

your job tricky. Frank discussions with groups of employees may help to manage such situations and prevent humor from becoming contentious.

- Monitor your own humor use and keep it fairly safe. Jobs have been lost over getting this wrong.
- Keep in mind that subordinates who laugh along with your joke may be doing this as a response to your power, or out of embarrassment, rather than out of genuine amusement.
- Humor is one way that employees can resist managerial control. Although humor about the organization and/or its management does not change the underlying workplace dynamics, it can allow employees a 'voice' to 'push back' without being openly hostile. Be sensitive to resistance humor and acknowledge the employees' perspective that underlies the joke.
- The dark side of humor ranges from mild insubordination to full blown aggression and harassment, wrapped up in a joke format. You must work out when to discipline transgressors; when to gently remind and admonish; and when to simply 'let it go'.
- Workplace sessions about what is, and is not, 'ok' may prevent humor becoming a workplace issue. Humor training has the potential for camaraderie, fun, laughter and good attendance. This could be handled in-house by an astute manager or HR representative, or alternatively there are workplace consultants offering humor seminars to the corporate sector.

CHAPTER 10

Managing Humor

In this our final chapter, we focus on the *management* of workplace humor. In the preceding chapters—particularly Chaps. 8 and 9, we have seen the best and the worst that humor can do. At the end of each chapter except the first one we have provided 'takeaways'—bite-sized pieces of advice about what organizational members, particularly managers, can do to 'get it right' in relation to humor. Here, we try to consolidate our material.

Managing humor, as we discussed in Chap. 8, is sometimes a matter, particularly in a relatively humorless organization, of promoting humor. In that chapter and in Chap. 6 (on 'managed fun'), we discussed small steps that managers can take to give humor a boost. Our advice, however, was to take such initiatives gently and not to make them at all compulsory.

The more common problem, however, is that of *controlling* humor; ensuring that humor is of a type and at a level that promotes good feelings and high morale, and avoids offensiveness and ill feeling. Here, we return to the idea of *humor boundaries* that we first explored in Chap. 3. If humor has these boundaries, where is the 'border control'? Who 'patrols' the boundary, and what mechanisms are there to bring those who cross the boundaries into line? The answer is, we all do!

Remember the taxonomy of humor participants we identified in Chap. 1?

- Humorists (or 'jokers'): those who most commonly initiate workplace humor (see Chap. 7)

© The Author(s) 2019
B. Plester, K. Inkson, *Laugh out Loud: A User's Guide to Workplace Humor*, https://doi.org/10.1007/978-981-13-0283-1_10

- Targets: those to whom, or at whom, humor—including both friendly banter and hostile ridicule—is directed, and who sometimes become 'victims'
- Observers (or 'audience')—those who are neither jokers not targets but who hear, see and sometimes respond to workplace humor
- Informal gatekeepers—those who take informal responsibility for guarding and/or changing organizational norms and standards of humor
- Formal gatekeepers—those, often in Human Resource departments, who have formal responsibility for organizational policies that may affect the use of humor in the organization
- Managers—those with formal responsibility for, and authority over, a group, team, or department, including authority over its use of humor

Each of these has a role to play in the management of humor. And each, we believe, can best conceptualize and discharge that role through consideration of the boundaries to humor in that particular situation (Chap. 3). Was the humor within the boundaries of the acceptable? If so, there is presumably no problem. If the humor was outside these boundaries, how does one respond? Here, we have specific suggestions to make to each group. Basically, these suggestions are not just about taking remedial action on humor that falls outside the boundaries, but in some cases also about *moving the boundaries.*

JOKERS

The problem of humor boundary control for jokers is that their natural tendency is to want to 'push the boundaries'. While, as in the case of 'Banana Time' (Chap. 5), workers can find endless repetitions of the same joke endlessly amusing, in most cases jokes repeated too often lose their luster and become boring. To retain their appeal to their audiences, jokers often find they must develop new material. This can be done by taking advantage of changes in the environment, for example a new system, a new employee, a new event, or even a colleague's new hairdo or outfit. However, new humor can also be developed by making new jokes about the same things, talking in a new way, perhaps a riskier way, being more 'edgy' in their humor.

Jokers will usually find that humor in contemporary organizations is fraught with sensitivities and taboos built into the wider culture about what is considered 'politically correct'. In many workplaces, sexist, sexual, racist, ageist, aggressive or 'bad taste' jokes are either informally controlled or subject to the formal rules and sanctions of management. Jokers often find that the possibility of potential disapproval limits their natural exuberance (or indeed, underneath it, their natural sexuality or vulgarity or aggression or prejudice, see Chaps. 2 and 7). Being the joker enables them to extend humor boundaries by indulging in risky behavior, but they need to be sensitive to the potential and actual response from others.

Taking It one Step Further
Mac, the 'tummy-banging' joker mentioned earlier, set up a 'tummy bang' with his colleague where they went one stage further: he and his partner in the joke pulled up their business shirts so that their naked paunches were exposed during the prank. And after it was over, Mac announced, 'And now we'll play all-boy nudie leapfrog!'

What do we make of Mac's 'edgy' humor in these situations? Are they harmlessly funny? Or were their pranks offensive behavior, even sexual harassment? As Mac himself says, part of his role is 'pushing the boundaries'. In both the shirt-opening and the remark about 'nudie leap-frog', Mac is breaking new humor ground in his organization by behaving and talking in a way that some might possibly find offensive. No one did, so Mac had perhaps succeeded in extending the humor boundary of his company. His joke seems relatively harmless. Mac is a smart joker: he pushes the boundary only at the margins, with gags that are only just outside the likely norm; and he pays attention to how targets, observers, and gatekeepers react. Management is nervous about Mac's antics, but so far he has given them no reason to intervene.

On the other hand, we have provided plenty of examples in this book of jokers who went just one step too far beyond the boundary: the man who leaped out of a wheelie bin when his boss was there; the new employee who unwittingly made a 'disabled' joke to the mother of a child with a disability; the 'G-string Friday' manager who lost his job. So our advice to jokers is as follows:

> First of all, are you sure you are the right person to be the joker? You may think you are funny, but do others laugh, and if they do, do they mean it? Think carefully before throwing yourself enthusiastically into the joker role. Try to share the role of joker, perhaps with an 'offsider' who can assist, and at time substitute for, the joker. Don't get competitive with other jokers.

Make sure that you know and understand your own work context, its professional norms, standards and where boundaries lie for humor. Get to know your colleagues. Understand their sensitivities so that you can avoid their 'no go' areas. Err on the side of caution, at least in your public displays. Be sensitive to mood: avoid trying to be too funny on somber occasions. When you get it wrong, and it is likely that you will at some stage, apologize immediately, unreservedly and authentically to all those you have offended. Discuss with your manager if necessary. Don't hide your gaffe behind more humor. Take it quietly for a while.

Be aware of the impact of the joker role on your own personal image or brand. Being the 'joker' may mean that you are not taken seriously and not a candidate for promotion. Be aware that adding responsibility may limit your ability to use humor. Which role would you prefer?

Re-read the other 'takeaways for jokers' at the conclusion of Chap. 7.

Targets/Victims

What about responses to humor that is not directed generally, but at *you:* humor that goes beyond the normal, friendly and acceptable banter that we described in Chap. 4 but seems, by chance or by the joker's design, to mock, ridicule, or humiliate you, as indicated in Chap. 9.

- 'Thanks for pointing out the error, dear. We haven't all got degrees from fucking Harvard, you know.'
- 'Don't worry, no one will say a word, the way you've got your nose up the boss's backside. Know what I mean, ha-ha?'
- 'It's ok, leave her alone, she's always the last to catch on.'

Here's a true story:

What Do You Say to That?

Blanche is an award-winning English journalist who has been commissioned by an international magazine to write a story about an Australian bush reserve, replete with native animals and doing pioneering conservation work. She has an accompanying renowned photographer, anxious to get good shots of both the staff and the wildlife. Bruno, the head of the reserve, is concerned that the journalists' intrusion may upset both the staff and the animals. He would rather the story not go ahead but has been instructed by his Board that the favorable international publicity that the reserve will get from the story, and likely downstream funding, mean that Blanche and the photographer must be accommodated.

How can the two sides work together? Bruno, a straight-laced, no-nonsense Australian, decides on some ground rules that he thinks the journalist and photography team should follow. He calls a meeting in his office involving his senior staff as well as Blanche and her people.

Bruno opens the meeting. Quietly and earnestly he outlines the problem and suggests a way to proceed. He is in mid-sentence when Blanche interrupts, with a huge smile:

'Oh, Bruno, do sit down! You shit-and-sawdust sheep-shaggers always think we journos don't know how to behave around animals. Well, I'm the horse whisperer incarnate. I've charmed more mammals and marsupials than you've had blow jobs, my lovely, so don't worry about it!'

This is an admittedly extreme example of workplace humor. While the words sound insulting, the smile assures Bruno that it's a jokey way of putting things. But how will Bruno react? How *should* he react? If *you* were Bruno, how would you react? Here are some possibilities.

1. Laugh heartily. It's a really funny remark and she has 'broken the ice'.
2. Ignore the intervention and get back to the point.
3. Frown or screw up your face to show your disgust and contempt for such insults and language.

4. Convey outrage, for example 'Please moderate your language! This is a serious problem!' or even 'How dare you accuse me of perverted practices?'
5. Try to give as good as you get, for example 'Well, my scientists have had it up to here with arty-farty media types who don't know a dolphin from a dingo!'
6. Just stand there (as Bruno did) with your jaw hanging open, unable to deal with the situation

We don't recommend any of these responses particularly. Our point is that a target of humor, like an observer of humor, is never a mere recipient of humor but always a *responder* to humor, even if that response is to stand there, like Bruno, looking too shocked to speak. And your response, whatever it is, will often either reinforce the humor as being within acceptable boundaries—at least your personal boundary (responses 1 and possibly 5 above), or will declare that it is outside the boundary (responses 2, 3 and 4)—in which case you are implicitly attempting to *shift* the boundary.

The situation is complicated by the power dynamics involved. Who holds the most power here, Blanche or Bruno? Bruno is head of the reserve, but he has been instructed by his superiors that Blanche's visit is very important and must be accommodated. Being as rude to her as she has been to him may jeopardize the whole deal. And should Bruno wish to complain, who would he complain to? Blanche is self-employed. A powerful humorist is harder to deal with than a subordinate. In this case, where the relationship between Blanche and Bruno will last only a few days, Option 2 ('move on') is probably the best one.

'It Was Only a Joke!'

One of the hardest things for joke victims to overcome is the habitual defense, 'but it was only a joke' or 'we were just having a bit of fun', or 'I didn't *mean* it' (with the unspoken implication, 'How could you be stupid enough to think I did?'). For the victim, these remarks only make things worse, by implying that s/he is oversensitive and lacking in a sense of humor. And yes, although it seems that almost totally humorless people do exist, nearly everybody *does* have a sense of humor: it's just that everyone has a different sense of humor, and what A finds supremely funny may be totally unfunny to B, particularly if B is the 'butt' of the 'joke'.

Here's a plaintive blogger with a 'victim of humor' problem:

Your Trouble Is, You Have No Sense of Humor

'I'm sure everyone knows the situation where someone offends you, and you tell them so, and they say 'you have no sense of humor' or 'I am only joking' but then keep right on saying the unfunny insults over and over. ... I have tried saying 'well you may be right about that' and then leave it at that, but it didn't work. It's a work situation and he has a position of authority over me. He basically needles me all the time, and when I tell him that I don't like it and I'd prefer not to chat, he comes back with the same every time, 'I was JOKING!' We used to be friends, but now I can't stand him. How do I get through a few more months of this constant crap?'

The blogger asks readers to suggest appropriate responses. Here are a few.

'Simply break out laughing in one of those 100% phony Ha-Ha-Ha types of laugh, or even better, show no sign of smile and go Hee-Hee-Hee as loud as you can.'

'Laugh loudly and for an uncomfortably long time. Then stop abruptly and stare at the person for three seconds.'

'Say, 'I have no sense of humor? You have a very small dick'.'

But is that the best we can do? Tit-for-tat? Responses such as these, we feel, are tackling offensive humor with more offensive humor. The first two seek to disconcert and/or insult the joker, who is most likely to shake his head, laugh and say contemptuously 'What a nut-case!' The third is countering an insult with a bigger insult. All these responses will likely escalate the situation, and broaden rather than narrow the humor boundaries. And if, as seems likely the original joker is a more aggressive humorist than the victim, then he or she will most likely win.

We quite like the more straightforward

Joker: 'You have no sense of humor!'
Victim: 'No, you're just not very funny.'

But even there, the objective of the victim seems to be to 'win' over the joker, in a way that is likely to promote further retaliation and will not solve the problem or move the boundary. Surely we can do better than that!

Occasionally the victim of humor is smart enough to come up with a quick riposte that silences the joker and, as it were, settles the argument. Here's our favorite example:

Tina and the Ambulance crew
At Victory TV, Tina is a highly experienced producer in her mid-50s, known for ruling with a steely grip and not kowtowing to anyone. It is her first day in charge of a hospital documentary series where her team will be working (and filming) with a group of (entirely male) ambulance crew. She is heading to the ambulance crew's break room, where they spend any time between calls or on breaks—the scene of much banter. The ambulance boys in there, have already spent a couple of hours teasing Tina's young researcher and director who have arrived earlier that day. It is clear they thought there was a lot of mileage to be had out of teasing these earnest young TV people.

As Tina arrived, one of the ambulance officers turns to another and says—very loudly—'Well, you know what I always say mate—women are only good for two things—fucking and making the coffee'. At this—Tina turned toward the man who had said it and said, very slowly,—'I. DON'T. MAKE. COFFEE'. The rest of the ambulance crew burst out laughing, and the man who'd said it bowed his head, thoroughly chastened....

In such situations, most of us are less quick-witted than Tina, and it is probably better to make no response than a feeble one. But if you are the victim there are other steps you can take. There are forms of conflict *resolution* quite distinct from the method of conflict *escalation* implied by the responses to the blogger we mentioned earlier.

Here, we summarize arguments made by Amy Gallo, in a *Harvard Business Review* article entitled 'How to respond to an offensive comment at work'.

Imagine that the remark a colleague has made makes you feel uncomfortable. He thinks he's just being funny, but the comment is inappropriate—maybe even offensive, sexist or racist. What should you say or do? Was the remark 'just a joke' in which you should join, or was it deliberately offensive? How can you avoid putting the other person on the defensive? And if you protest, are you taking a risk, particularly if the other person is a superior in the organization?

Usually the benefits of speaking up outweigh the disadvantages. If you don't speak up, you're signaling that this is OK. You agree that what has been said is within your acceptable boundary. You're encouraging offensive behavior. But you also need to think about the specifics of the situation. Was the offensive joke an example of a habit, or was it a one-off? Does the person behave the same way with others? Does the behavior seem to be intentional or merely thoughtless?

If you decide to take action, start by assuming that the other person offended you only inadvertently: they thought they were making a funny, innocent comment and didn't realize it would hurt. Accusations such as 'that's racist' just cause defensiveness. Rather (and this is a common piece of advice in for all manner of interpersonal conflicts, not just those about humor), explain how the joke made you *feel*, for example 'I know you didn't mean it, but it made me feel incompetent'. This may sound a little 'touchy-feely', but the research suggests it is the approach most likely to change behavior. A follow-up technique may be to ask what they meant when they made their comment. Discussion may assist them to understand their biases and realize the effects of their words on others.

Of course, you may decide that the person really does 'have it in' for you, or is totally alienated from the organization (see section on humor as resistance, Chap. 9), or is so prejudiced that intervention of the type suggested here is likely to do more harm than good. At this point, you may consider escalating the issue.

If the needling is maintained to a point where you feel harassed or bullied to an extent where your well-being is threatened, it may be worth starting to keep a diary of instances and eventually advise the joker that if the behavior continues you will be sending a formal complaint to higher authority, accompanied by your record. You may even want to go 'the whole hog' and actually send in the complaint. In today's growing climate of non-tolerance of offensive (particularly sexual, sexist, homophobic and racist) workplace behavior, there is an increasing chance that your organization will be sympathetic and will have policies and procedures in place to deal with the problem.

Also, there is power in numbers. If someone's humor offends you, it's likely to have offended others. You might simultaneously seek support and corroboration from other workers who may also have been offended and make the case that the person is creating a hostile climate not just for you, but for many others, perhaps even for the whole department or organization.

OBSERVERS

Observers not directly involved in humor but witnessing it can also make a difference. Jokers are encouraged when those around them smile or laugh at their antics. Often, your laughter will be a spontaneous response to something you find funny, but in other cases you will find the material either unfunny or even offensive, and will be laughing merely because others are, to be 'part of the crowd'. This response is unintentionally deceptive, and jokers cannot be blamed for thinking that you like their humor. The humor climate in an organization is healthiest when people respond honestly.

Of particular interest is the response of 'unlaughter'—deliberately not laughing and putting on a neutral or even slightly disapproving expression in a situation which someone else considers to be funny or where others around you are laughing. If you think the humor boundaries have been stretched too far, unlaughter can be a good way to make your point.

As an observer who finds the humor offensive, you may decide that even though you are not a direct target of the humor, you are a victim: if so, the steps suggested in the previous section may also apply to you.

GATEKEEPERS

Gatekeepers need sensitivity: they need to be able to identify when someone's humor is likely to be distracting or offensive or otherwise beyond the organization's norms. They need to be willing to intervene actively on such occasions. They also need authority, which can be either the authority of their formal position or the authority they carry as respected members of staff. When they identify humor that goes too far, they need to be listened to with respect and to have their advice followed.

Informal Gatekeepers

This doesn't have to involve 'waving a big stick': a respected boss or senior employee can easily deliver an admonition or warning quietly and personally, perhaps even with a smile. Our observations of effective human 'gatekeeping' include many instances of rank-and-file employees stepping in to prevent minor breaches of the informal code, thus preserving the boundary not by self-conscious managerial formality but by small-scale good-natured finger-wagging. Here are two examples:

Keep the Party Clean, Boys!
Edith, a 50-plus-year-old long-service, respected legal secretary at Kapack, the conservative law firm we described in Chap. 3, heard some ribald laughter. Looking round, she saw some male colleagues sharing a joke about some risqué humor which had been sent to one of them by email. She caught a glimpse of some sexual images on a computer screen. Both the laughter and the images were outside the normal boundaries at Kapack. So Edith got up, walked over to the group and said, 'Keep the party clean, boys!' The men looked embarrassed, muttered apologies and dispersed.

At Adare, the no-boundaries-humor IT company, two female workers, Ann and Rachel, decided that although they enjoyed most of the fun and games and even lewd humor that CEO Jake practiced and encouraged, they needed some protection from the more extreme forms. So they made it clear that as far as physical jokes such as 'missile fights' were concerned, they were off-limits and that should any missiles used in Adare's pranks and horseplay hit either of them, the perpetrators would be expected to compensate them with a bottle of wine. Even in zany Adare, they made their point. We subsequently observed a 'humorous' incident in which the male employees threw sausage rolls and cakes all over the office space, but none went anywhere near Rachel or Ann.

In the first case, Edith's intervention is probably effective because of her status in the organization as a senior, long-service respected employee. That isn't inevitable: in Chap. 3 we described the case of Brenda, a woman of similar age to Edith, who faced with a similar situation, intervened as a gatekeeper on only her second day in the organization, resulting not in change of the humor boundaries but in her ostracism from her work group. Gatekeeping is only for those with the necessary 'weight' in the organization.

Informal gatekeeping may also work in the short term but not in the long term. The young lawyers admonished by Edith stopped their sleazy joking immediately and walked away: but did they change their behavior? What did they think privately? 'Oops—we crossed the line and got caught, better not do that again' or 'Silly old bag, why doesn't she mind her own business?' Successful gatekeeping depends on respect both for the organization's conventions and for the gatekeeper.

The second incident above ('no food fights near us') shows that to some extent, as far as physical factors permit, individuals can, if they wish, 'opt out' of some aspects of the prevalent humor culture, that is, observers can become gatekeepers, at least of their own space. They can say, for example, 'Tell these jokes if you like, but please not where I can hear them!' or 'Leave me off the list for funny emails please'. In these cases, the humor culture is undisturbed, and the humorists may even like the fact that those who are most likely to dislike the joke will not be involved in it. But of course total protection of individuals is often impossible. Some readers might find the very idea of throwing food around intolerable in any organization for which they work, even if they aren't personally involved. But if they work at Adare they will have to put up with it, or leave.

Formal Gatekeeping

In other cases, perhaps where the breach of norms is serious, repeated, or collective, HR managers and others must use their formal authority plus the respect that others have for them, to enact the gatekeeping role. In cases such as the jumping-out-of-a-wheelie-bin prank that went wrong (Chap. 4), the HR department, thought of in some organizations as the 'Humor Police', can be coopted as gatekeepers. They may be able to point out formally and sternly that the behavior in question is outside the organization's rules and must not be repeated.

We found in our research that most HR managers sooner or later get involved in the policing of humor. HR managers tend to know more than other workers and managers about the negative consequences that can flow from the crossing of humor boundaries. And the fact that HR is doing the formal disciplining and is independent from the employee's own work group, may help the group's manager to avoid any subsequent hostility from the staff. Here, the 'good cop' group manager perhaps uses his or her informal relationship with the miscreant to balance the 'bad cop' HR manager or senior manager who imposes formal discipline.

Nevertheless, it is probably best for managers to try and avoid the crossing of humor boundaries to such an extent that higher authority, rules, regulations and sanctions have to be invoked. There is, after all, something free-spirited, creative and liberating about much humor, such that any formal action perceived to control and limit it risks 'throwing out the baby with the bathwater', controlling and squeezing out more and more of employees' personality and spontaneity and leading to accusations of 'PC police', 'blue meanies', 'spoilsports' and so on. That is certainly the way some staff will perceive the formal policing of humor: overkill conducted by petty bureaucrats.

MANAGERS

In any work group, team, department or whole organization, there will be a manager who has formal authority and takes formal responsibility for all the group's activities and behavior. Potentially, though perhaps within the limits set by the wider organization, these men and women have the most crucial role to play in determining the group's overall and humor culture, setting its humor boundaries, and encouraging or discouraging and in extreme cases, disciplining different forms and instances of humor. There will of course be cases, such as in the 'resistance' call center cultures we described in Chap. 9, where humor has slipped, along with many other aspects of culture, beyond managers' control. Here, any improvement of the organization's humor culture must evolve as a by-product of much more general and substantial organization change.

However, our research also suggested that in most organizations employees recognize the authority of the organization to set the standards. In our interviews with them, many employees saw humor at work as an issue of managerial authority and permission. Thus:

> 'They do encourage the whole fun thing, but there is a definite line there and much as we do joke it is still very professional.'
> 'There are some things that aren't appropriate (in incoming electronic media) but then again they still let us have a bit of fun.'
> 'They'll certainly hand out the fun themselves which is kind of fun. But if you think you can do something that's inappropriate, they'll smack your hand.'

The imagery is very much of potentially naughty children uneasily recognizing the role of their parents in setting boundaries for them. They want their parents to make sure they have a good time, but also to be able to step in smartly to control things if the party shows signs of getting out of hand.

In the 'takeaways' at the end of Chaps. 2, 3, 4, 5, 6, 7, 8 and 9 of this book we have focused on takeaways for managers, so at this point it is perhaps best to repeat some of the key messages. For this section, we assume the reader is a manager.

In Chap. 2 (How humor works), we emphasized the *background knowledge* role of managers in managing humor. You should know the context, including the people, their issues, attitudes and relationships, the history of the situation and the surrounding culture. You should have some understanding of the theories of humor and its various psychological bases as described in the chapter. You should observe the humor behavior in the group, including being able to notice how staff are responding to the humor, for example noticing 'unlaughter'. You should be able to determine the humor that is healthy and productive and that which may lead to ill-feeling and conflict.

In Chap. 3 (Humor and organization culture), we described different organizational and group cultures with huge differences in the types of humor they encourage and their humor boundaries. We noted that managers play a major part in determining these cultures and boundaries. Here, the manager's powers of observation are key. Be savvy about what will, and will not, be tolerated, in terms of both formal rules and informal culture. Note whether humor is formally or informally controlled in the organization, and whether there are subcultures with their own norms. Know your own organization's policies and rules. If you are able, get some of your staff to complete (anonymously) the Humor Climate Questionnaire that we provide, to try and diagnose some of the positive and negative features of your humor culture. Pay special attention to the way newcomers are socialized into the organization's culture: look after them. Lastly, try to ensure that your own humor is congruent with the overall culture that your organization has established.

In Chap. 4, we covered various common forms of humor, including banter, canned jokes, pranks and horseplay, and showed some of their upsides and downsides. Do what you can to ensure that staff understand the sensitivities of colleagues before their jokes go too far, and people need to avoid telling jokes that might cause offence. Take care with pranks: never conduct or condone a prank that has health or safety risks or breaches your organization's staff policies.

In Chap. 5 we looked at humor rituals such as ceremonies, presentations and staff outings, including 'managed fun' events funded and organized by the organization. Such events may not be your 'cup of tea', but if you are a manager we think you should, as far as you feel able, join in with the humor/fun activities that you don't feel uncomfortable with. If you have values that you feel should be promoted, or people who you think should be honored, try to be creative in developing planned events, involving elements of humor, that would do that. But before organizing fun events, do try to determine how popular they are likely to be. A 'social committee' able to sound out staff and organize events accordingly is often a good idea. Modify the nature of the fun to suit employees' tastes. Avoid any suggestion that such events are compulsory, or that non-attendees are 'spoilsports' or 'wet blankets'.

In Chap. 6, we considered the influence of modern technology such as email, social media and viral jokes on workplace humor. Our takeaways were largely for staff and emphasized the need to be careful in entrusting potentially risky material to the tender mercies of the Internet. They need to be vigilant about the content and recipients of their communications, their social media postings, their handling of commercially sensitive or potentially embarrassing material about the organization and the material that is on public display on their screens. As a manager it is up to you not just to follow such simple principles yourself but also to communicate the standards to your team.

In Chap. 7, we looked at the special role that habitual organizational jokers play in workplace humor. Here, you should seek to identify the joker, recognize the potential importance of the role, appraise the joker's input, and if it seems to have positive value, treasure it. Make it clear if there are topics or forms of humor that are 'off limits'. When the joker 'crosses the line' and upsets someone with their humor, a private warning may be necessary in the context of recognition of their positive humor contributions. Assuming the joker's popularity, involve them in planning social or fun events. Involve them in any discussions of workplace policies around humor.

Chapter 8 is about the bright side of humor. Here, you should aim to recognize the morale, social and health benefits that humor can bring. Encourage and promote humor where there seems to be too little but ensure it doesn't go too far in terms of either disruption of work or causing offence to some employees. You can reinforce the kind of humor culture you want by encouragement and even incentives for staff (e.g. laughing when a staff member is genuinely funny, giving positive feedback, offering funding for appropriate social events). You need to be aware, however, of bad or unpopular would-be-be jokers. A gentle but kind word may be necessary to reduce this effect but should be coupled with recognition of the humorist's value and good intentions.

In Chap. 9, we focused the dark side of humor, the damaging expression through humor of underlying traits and attitudes such as aggression, sexual frustration, and gender- and race-based hostility. If this is an issue, you will have to take responsibility for policing it. You should be aware of relevant company policies and rules. You will need to monitor your own humor and ensure it shows no hint of the types of humor you want to keep out. You need to ensure your staff are aware of the standards required, and if there is a problem you may need to convene meetings to manage and improve the situation. You may want to call in formal gatekeepers such as the HR department to reinforce your message. In extreme cases, disciplinary action may be necessary.

CONCLUSION

We have come to the end of our excursion through workplace humor. We have suggested how humor works psychologically. We have shown how workplace humor is essentially a by-product or dimension of organization culture. We have shown how people 'do' humor, the main workplace forms of humor and the organizational rituals in which it is infused. We have considered the revolutionary effect of digital technology on the nature and propagation of humor. We have drawn special attention to organizational jokers, the lynchpins of workplace humor, and shown how, and why, they operate. We have demonstrated humor's liberating 'bright side' at work, its potential for boosting good feeling, morale and even staff health; and the dark side, where humor, sometimes unintentionally, has malicious and destructive effects. Finally, in this chapter, we have tried to suggest a few strategies and actions that everyone—jokers, targets, observers, gatekeepers and managers—can use to get humor right in their organization.

Our book contrasts with other books, articles and websites we have read on the management of workplace humor. Where these other media are on the whole relentlessly positive about humor, we take a more cautious view, being perhaps more aware of the harm that ill-conceived humor can do. We believe work should be fun, but because of the ambiguity about what is fun and what is funny, attempts at humor so often go wrong. We also think that our view is in line with changing times, with the increasing role of women in the workplace, recognition of minority groups and human rights for freedom from offensive material and bullying.

From our own experience we know how good it can be to work in organizations where humor 'knows its place', and is clean, clever, positive and pleasurable. We hope this book has done something to make it so for you.

Appendix: Humor Climate Questionnaire (HCQ)—Scoring Key

When you calculate your scores on the Humor Climate Questionnaire (HCQ), remember that the results are indicative but not definitive. There are many sources of error to the scores. In particular, your questionnaire indicates only your own perception. Others in your organization may perceive things very differently. To check the reliability of your scores, you might ask others in your organization to compete the HCQ independently and check the average scores and range of scores.

This questionnaire measures four dimensions of Humor Culture.

The first dimension is called *Positive Humor.* In organizations high on this dimension humor is used socially in a positive way, to support others and strengthen relationships. To measure your organization's Positive Humor, add the scores for items 1, 8, 12 and 16. The score should be between 4 and 28.

The second dimension is *Negative Humor.* In organizations high on this dimension, humor is used to demean and belittle others. To measure your organization's Negative Humor, add the scores for items 5, 9, 11 and 14. The score should be between 4 and 28.

The third dimension is *Out-group Humor.* In organizations high on this dimension, humor is directed outside the group at another target, in this case higher-level management. To measure your organization's Out-group Humor, add the scores for items 2, 4, 6 and 13. The score should be between 4 and 28.

The fourth and last dimension *is Supervisor Support.* In organizations high on this dimension, humor is supported and encouraged by staff

© The Author(s) 2019

B. Plester, K. Inkson, *Laugh out Loud: A User's Guide to Workplace Humor*, https://doi.org/10.1007/978-981-13-0283-1

members' supervisors. The items that constitute this dimension actually indicate *lack of support*, so the scoring needs to be reversed. Add the scores for the remaining items, 3, 7, 10 and 15. Then subtract the total from 32. The score should be between 4 and 28.

What do the numbers mean? Well, you can compare your scores with those of an independent sample of 572 workers tested by Professor Cann and his colleagues. Their mean scores were as follows

Positive humor	21.1
Negative humor	13.1
Out-group humor	16.9
Supervisor support	20.7

By comparing your scores with those 'norms' and seeing whether they are above or below average on each dimension you can get an idea of how your organization appears to rate in comparison to others. However, we stress that these results are indicative only.

References, Notes and Further Reading

Chapter 1

For the case involving the prank at the ski fields, see:

The New Zealand Herald (2017) *Job prank drives out pregnant woman.* (http://www.nzherald.co.nz/nz/news/article.cfm?c_id=1&objectid=11922846, September 17, 2017).

In this chapter we refer to humor studies written by academics from different disciplinary fields. They follow grouped according to discipline:

Literary studies:

Charles, L. H. (1945). The clown's function. *The Journal of American Folklore, 58*(227), 25–34.

Evans, R. C. (1996). Forgotten fools: Alexander Barclay's *Ship of Fools.* In C. Davidson (Ed.), *Fools and folly.* Michigan: Western Michigan University.

Fry, W. F. J., & Allen, M. (1976). Humour as a creative experience: The development of a Hollywood humorist. In A. J. Chapman & H. C. Foot (Eds.), *Humour and laughter: Theory, research and applications,* 245–258. London: John Wiley & Sons.

© The Author(s) 2019
B. Plester, K. Inkson, *Laugh out Loud: A User's Guide to Workplace Humor*, https://doi.org/10.1007/978-981-13-0283-1

Happe, P. (1996). Staging folly in the early sixteenth century: Heywood, Lindsay, and others. In C. Davidson (Ed.), *Fools and folly*, pp. 285–301. Michigan: Western Michigan University.

Kivy, P. (2003). Jokes are a laughing matter. *The Journal of Aesthetics and Art Criticism, 61*(1), 515.

Anthropological studies:

Apte, M. L. (1985). *Humor and laughter: An anthropological approach*. Ithaca, N.Y. : Cornell University Press.

Radcliffe-Brown, A. R. (1940). On joking relationships. *Africa: Journal of the International African Institute, 13*(3), 195–210.

Sociological studies:

Billig, M. (2005). *Laughter and ridicule. Towards a social critique of humour*. London: Sage.

Davies, C. (1982). Ethnic jokes, moral values and social boundaries. *The British Journal of Sociology, 33*(3), 383–403.

Kuipers, G. (2011). "Where was King Kong when we needed him?" Public discourse, digital disaster jokes, and the functions of laughter after 9/11. In Ted Gournelos and Viveca Green, *A decade of dark humor: How comedy, irony and satire shaped post-9/11 America*. University Press of Mississippi: Mississippi.

Linstead, S. (1985). Jokers wild: The importance of humour in the maintenance of organisational culture. *Sociological Review, 13*(3), 741–767.

Lockyer, S. & Pickering, M. (2005). *Beyond a joke. The limits of humour*. Palgrave Macmillan: Hampshire.

Zigderveld, A. (1983). The sociology of humour and laughter. *Current Sociology, 31*(3).

Psychological studies:

Freud, S. (1905). *Jokes and their relation to the unconscious*. (A. Richards, Trans. 1991). London: Penguin.

Fisher, S., & Fisher, R. L. (1983). Personality and psychopathology in the comic. In P. E. McGhee & J. H. Goldstein (Eds.), *Handbook of humor research*, (*Vol. 2*). pp. 41–60 New York: Springer-Verlag.

Grotjahn, M. (1966). *Beyond laughter: Humor and the subconscious*. New York: McGraw-Hill

Martin, R. A. (2007). *The psychology of humor. An integrative approach.* Burlington, MA: Elsevier.

Mc Graw, P. A. & Warren, C. (2010). Benign violations: making immoral behaviour funny. *Association for Psychological Science, 21*(8), 1141–1149.

Provine, R. (2000). *Laughter: A scientific investigation.* London: Penguin.

Linguistic studies:

Attardo, S. (1997). The semantic foundations of cognitive theories of humor. *Humor, International Journal of Humor Research, 4*(10), 293–347.

Attardo, S. (2001). *Humorous texts: A semantic and pragmatic analysis.* New York: Walter de Gruyter.

Hay, J. (2000). Functions of humor in the conversations of men and women. *Journal of Pragmatics, 32*(6), 709–742.

Holmes, J. (2000). Politeness, power and provocation: How humour functions in the workplace. *Discourse Studies, 2*(2), 159–185.

Holmes, J., & Stubbe, M. (2003). *Power and politeness in the workplace: A sociolinguistic analysis of talk at work.* London: Longman.

Norrick, N. R. (2001). On the conversational performance of narrative jokes: Toward an account of timing. *Humor. International Journal of Humor Research, 14*(3), 255–274.

Raskin, V. (1985). *Semantic mechanisms of humor.* Dordrecht: D. Reidel.

Schnurr, S. & Plester, B. (2017). Functionalist Discourse Analysis of Humor. In Salvatore Attardo, (Ed.,) *Routledge Handbook of Language and Humor.* New York & London: Routledge

Barbara's academic book is discussed in this chapter:

Plester, B. A (2016). *The complexity of workplace humour: Laughter, jokers and the dark side.* Dordrecht: Springer.

We refer to books written on management and humor. Here are a few titles that we accessed:

Beaton, A. *The Little Book of Management Bollocks.* London: Simon & Schuster.

Gostick, A. & Christopher, S. (2008). *The Levity Effect.* New Jersey: Wiley.

Sathyanarayana, K. *The Power of Humor at the Workplace.* India: Sage

For further reading on banter at work, see:

Plester, B.A., & Sayers, J. G. (2007). Taking the piss: The functions of banter in three ITC companies. *Humor. International Journal of Humor Research, 20*(2) 157–187.

CHAPTER 2

The Big Bang Theory excerpt:

Chitti, S. (2013). *What are some of the funniest jokes in a television series?* Quora. com. (https://www.quora.com/What-are-some-of-the-funniest-jokes-in-a-television-series).

For further reading on 'hostile humor', see:

Becker, A. B. (2012). Comedy types and political campaigns: The differential influence of other-directed hostile humor and self-ridicule on candidate evaluations. *Mass Communication and Society, 15*(6), 791–812.

For further reading on humor involving racial stereotypes, see work by the late Christie Davies:

Davies, C. (1982). Ethnic jokes, moral values and social boundaries. *The British Journal of Sociology, 33*(3), 383–403.

To view our example 'Laughing at Colbert':

The Late Show with Stephen Colbert. Published on Jul 28, 2017. *Stephen Takes A Front-Stab At Scaramucci's Phone Interview.* (https://www.youtube.com/watch?v=Cn_Mlwouwng)

For further reading about the main humor theories:

Michael Billig summarizes and critiques the main humor theories in this book: Billig, M. (2005). *Laughter and ridicule. Towards a social critique of humour.* London: Sage.

For further reading about incongruity theories of humor, see:

Attardo, S. (1997). The semantic foundations of cognitive theories of humor. *Humor: International Journal of Humor Research.*

Nerhardt, G. (1976). Incongruity and funniness: Towards a new descriptive model. In A. J. Chapman & H. C. Foot (Eds.), *Humour and laughter: Theory, research and applications,* 55–62. London: John Wiley & Sons.

Ritchie, G. (1999). *Developing the incongruity-resolution theory.* Paper presented at the AISB Symposium on Creative Language, Edinburgh, Scotland.

For further reading about superiority humor theories, see:

Duncan, W. J. (1985). The superiority theory of humor at work: Joking relation-ships as indicators of formal and informal status patterns in small, task-oriented groups. *Small Group Behavior, 16*(4), 556–564.

Gruner, C. R. (1997). *The game of humor. A comprehensive theory of why we laugh.* New Brunswick: Transaction Publishers.

La Fave, L., Haddad, J. & Maesen, W. A. (1976). Superiority, enhanced self-esteem and perceived incongruity humour theory. In A. J. Chapman & H. C. Foot (Eds.), *Humour and laughter: Theory, research and applications,* (pp. 63–92). London: John Wiley & Sons.

For psychological work pertaining to the relief and release theories, see:

Freud, S. (1905). *Jokes and their relation to the unconscious.* (A. Richards, Trans. 1991). London: Penguin.

Shurcliff, A. (1968). Judged humor, arousal, and the relief theory. *Journal of personality and social psychology, 8*(4p1), 360.

For further reading on relational humor, see:

Collinson, D. (1988). 'Engineering humour': Joking and conflict in shop-floor relations. *Organization Studies, 9,* 181–199.

Cooper, C. (2008). Elucidating the bonds of workplace humor: A relational model. *Human Relations, 61*(8), 1087–1115.

Romero, E.J. & Pescosolido, A. (2008). Humor and group effectiveness. *Human Relations, 61*(3), 395–418.

For further reading on Erving Goffman's work on dramaturgy, see:

Goffman, E. (2006). The presentation of self. *Life as theater: A dramaturgical sourcebook.*
Goffman, E. (1975). Role-distance. *Life as theater: A dramaturgical sourcebook,* 123–132.

CHAPTER 3

For further reading about how organizational culture influences humor boundaries and joking, see:

Linstead, S. (1985). Jokers wild: The importance of humour in the maintenance of organisational culture. *Sociological Review, 13*(3), 741–767.
Plester, B. A. (2009). Crossing the line: Boundaries of workplace humour and fun. *Employee Relations, 31*(6), 584–599.

For further reading about the humor-loving Adare company and their specific culture, see:

Plester, B. A. (2015). Take it like a man! Performing hegemonic masculinity through organizational humour. *ephemera, 15*(3), 537–559.

For 'measuring your organization's humor culture', we use the questionnaire developed by Arnie Cann, Amanda Watson and Elisabeth Bridgewater. They have kindly granted us permission to use and publish their questionnaire, and we acknowledge their contribution with profound thanks. The relevant references are:

Cann, A., Watson, A. J., & Bridgewater, E. A. (2014). Assessing humor at work: The humor climate questionnaire. *Humor, 27*(2), 307–323.
Blanchard, A. L., Stewart, O. J., Cann, A., & Follman, L. (2014). Making sense of humor at work. *The Psychologist-Manager Journal, 17*(1), 49–70. (https://doi.org/10.1037/mgr0000011)

CHAPTER 4

Our statistic about conversational humor comes from this psychological study carried out by two renowned humor researchers Rod Martin and Nicholas Kuipers:

Martin, R. A., & Kuiper, N.A. (1999). Daily occurrence of laughter: Relationships with age, gender and Type A personality. *Humor: International Journal of Humor Research, 12*(4), 355–384.

For further reading on workplace banter, see:

Plester, B.A., & Sayers, J. G. (2007). Taking the piss: The functions of banter in three ITC companies. *Humor. International Journal of Humor Research, 20*(2) 157–187.

We use the Oxford Dictionary for some definitions in the book. The version we use is the online version found at: (https://en.oxforddictionaries.com/)

For further reading on canned jokes, see:

Norrick, N. R. (2001). On the conversational performance of narrative jokes: Toward an account of timing. *Humor. International Journal of Humor Research, 14*(3), 255–274.

Plester, B. A (2016). Chapter 3: Execution of a joke: Types and function of humour. In: *The complexity of workplace humour: Laughter, jokers and the dark side*. Dordrecht: Springer.

Our definition of a prank comes from the online dictionary:

(http://www.dictionary.com/)

For further reading about the British TV show: *The Office*, see:

Gervais, R., & Merchant, S. (2002). *The office*. [Retrieved 27 August 2003, from (www.bbc.co.uk/comedy/theoffice/).]

For further reading on pranks and horseplay, see:

Smith, M. (1996). Prank. *American Folklore An Encyclopedia*, 1232–1235.
Marsh, M. (2015). On going too far. *The European Journal of Humour Research*, *2*(4), 126–139.
Plester, B. A (2016). *The complexity of workplace humour: Laughter, jokers and the dark side*. Dordrecht: Springer.

CHAPTER 5

Our definitions of 'ritual' and 'institutionalize' are taken from the Oxford Dictionary online version found at:

(https://en.oxforddictionaries.com/)

For further reading about organizational rituals, see:

Deal, T., & Kennedy, A. (1982). *Corporate cultures. The rites and rituals of corporate life*. London: Penguin. Note: This is a very well-known study popular with managers and academics.
Islam, G. & Zyphur, J. (2009). Rituals in organizations. A review and expansion of current theory. *Group & Organization Management, 34*(1), 114–139.

For further reading about hazing, see:

Festinger, L., & Carlsmith, J. M. (1959). Cognitive consequences of forced compliance. *The Journal of Abnormal and Social Psychology*, *58*(2), 203.
Joséfowtz, N. & Gadon, H. (1989). Hazing: Uncovering one of the best-kept secrets of the workplace. Business Horizons, 32(3), 22–26

For further reading about managed fun, see:

Plester, B.A. (2009). Crossing the line: Boundaries of workplace humour and fun. *Employee Relations, 31*(6), 584–599.
Plester, B. A., Cooper-Thomas, H. & Winquist, J. (2015). The fun paradox. *Employee Relations, 37(3)*, 380–398.

Plester, B. & Hutchison, A. (2016). Fun times: The relationship between fun and engagement. *Employee Relations, 38*(3), 332-350.

Our examples of workplace rituals came from this site:

(http://mikekerr.com/use-rituals-and-traditions-to-add-humor-to-work-and-motivate-employees-2/)

To read the full paper 'Banana time', see:

Roy, D. (1959). 'Banana Time': Job satisfaction and informal interaction. *Human Organisation Studies, 18*, 158–168.

CHAPTER 6

For information about Grumpy Cat ® and LOLcats, see:

Grumpy Cat ® (https://www.grumpycats.com/about)
I canhascheesburger? Animals. (http://icanhas.cheezburger.com/lolcats/tag/work)

For information about memes, see:

Flo Perry (2015). 28 Memes Everyone Who Works in an Office Will Understand (https://www.buzzfeed.com/floperry/memes-everyone-who-works-in-an-office-will-get?utm_term=.kyl8p3JLa#.qp89mM1vX)

For further reading on digital disaster jokes, see:

Kuipers, G. (2011). "Where was King Kong when we needed him?" Public discourse, digital disaster jokes, and the functions of laughter after 9/11. In Ted Gournelos and Viveca Green, *A decade of dark humor: How comedy, irony and satire shaped post-9/11 America*. University Press of Mississippi: Mississippi.

For further reading on emoji, see:

Emojipedia -Home of emoji meanings. (https://emojipedia.org/)

Alex Hern (2015). Don't know the difference between emoji and emoticons? Let me explain (https://www.theguardian.com/technology/2015/feb/06/difference-between-emoji-and-emoticons-explained)

For further reading on cyberloafing, see:

Lim, V. K. G. (2002). The IT way of loafing on the job: cyberloafing, neutralizing and organizational justice. *Journal of Organizational Behavior, 23*(5) 675–694.

Lim, V. K. G. & Chen, D.J.Q. (2012). Cyberloafing at the workplace: gain or drain on work? *Behaviour & Information Technology, 31*(4), 343–353.

For further reading on email and the workplace:

Chris Wright, (2016). *Email and the workplace.* (http://scitechconnect.elsevier.com/email-and-the-workplace/)

Shawn Smith, *Email in the Workplace: Avoiding Legal Landmines* (http://www.mediate.com/articles/smith.cfm)

Jacquelyn Smith, 15 Email Etiquette Rules Every Professional Should Follow (https://www.inc.com/business-insider/email-etiquette-rules.html)

(https://www.groovypost.com/howto/what-are-emojis-how-and-when-to-use-them/)

Radhika Sanghani (2016). Your boss can read your personal emails. Here's what you need to know. (http://www.telegraph.co.uk/women/work/your-boss-can-read-your-personal-emails-heres-what-you-need-to-k/)

Our social media examples of posting comments that caused issues, see:

Helen A.S. Popkin, (2009). Getting the skinny on Twitter's 'Cisco Fatty'. (http://www.nbcnews.com/id/29901380/ns/technology_and_science-tech_and_gadgets/t/getting-skinny-twitters-cisco-fatty/#.WrXD5kxuLD4)

Call-centre worker fairly dismissed for offensive Facebook comments about colleague:

Teggart v TeleTech UK Ltd NIIT/704/11 (http://www.xperthr.co.uk/editors-choice/call-centre-worker-fairly-dismissed-for-offensive-facebook-comments-about-colleague/112847/)

CHAPTER 7

For further reading about jokers and 'fools' both modern and traditional, see:

Charles, L. H. (1945). The clown's function. *The Journal of American Folklore,* 58(227), 25–34.

Evans, R. C. (1996). Forgotten fools: Alexander Barclay's *Ship of Fools.* In C. Davidson (Ed.), *Fools and folly.* Michigan: Western Michigan University.

Happe, P. (1996). Staging folly in the early sixteenth century: Heywood, Lindsay, and others. In C. Davidson (Ed.), *Fools and folly,* pp. 285–301.Michigan: Western Michigan University.

Kets de Vries, M. F. R. (1990). The organisational fool: Balancing a leader's hubris. *Human Relations, 43*(8), 751–770.

Plester, B. A. & Orams, M. B. (2008). Send in the clowns: The role of the joker in three New Zealand IT companies. *Humor. International Journal of Humour Research, 21*(3), 253–281.

For the excerpt from Shakespeare's *Twelfth Night,* see:

Shakespeare, W. (1975). *Twelfth night.* Cengage Learning EMEA.

For further reading about women's humor at work, see:

Holmes, J., Marra, M. & Burns, L. (2001). Women's humour in the workplace. A quantitative analysis. *Australian Journal of Communication, 28*(1), 83–108.

Plester, B. A. (2015). Take it like a man! Performing hegemonic masculinity through organizational humour. *ephemera, 15*(3), 537–559.

We again reference the UK version of *The Office* TV series:

Gervais, R., & Merchant, S. (2002). *The office.* [Retrieved 27 August 2003, from (www.bbc.co.uk/comedy/theoffice/).]

For further reading about the concept of 'unlaughter', see:

Billig, M. (2005). *Laughter and ridicule. Towards a social critique of humour.* London: Sage.

Butler, N. (2015). 'Joking aside: Theorizing laughter in organizations', *Culture and Organization*, 21(1), 42–58.

We note that the Roger Sutton incident was a true event. For articles related to the Roger Sutton workplace humor incident, see:

Martin Van Beynen & Hamish Rutherford (2014). *Roger Sutton and his dramatic downfall* (https://www.stuff.co.nz/national/politics/63891913/roger-sutton-and-his-dramatic-downfall)

Hamish Rutherford & Georgina Stylianou (2014). Cera boss Roger Sutton resigns over sexual harassment claims. (https://www.stuff.co.nz/business/better-business/63259777/Cera-boss-Roger-Sutton-resigns-over-sexual-harassment-claims)

Martin Van Beynen, (2014). *Roger Sutton resigns with regrets* (https://www.stuff.co.nz/business/industries/63292588/roger-sutton-resigns-with-regrets)

CHAPTER 8

To find lyrics to songs such as 'Always look on the bright side of life' and others mentioned in this chapter, we use Lyrics.com (https://www.lyrics.com/).

The quote discussing the man going to the gallows comes from an old essay of Freud's and can be accessed thus:

Freud, S. (1927, Humor. p.161 (https://www.scribd.com/doc/34515345/Sigmund-Freud-Humor-1927).

For further reading on positive effects of workplace humor, see:

Maon, F., & Lindgreen, A. (2018). How to take the joke, strategic uses and roles humor in counter-corporate social movements. In Maon, François; Lindgreen,

Adam; Vanhamme, Joelle; Angell, Robert; Memery, Juliet (eds.). *Not All Claps and Cheers: Humor in Business and Society Relationships*. Milton Park: Routledge.

Peebles, D., Martin, A., & Hecker, R. (2018). The value of positive humor in the workplace: enhancing work attitudes and performance. In, Maon, François; Lindgreen, Adam; Vanhamme, Joelle; Angell, Robert; Memery, Juliet (eds). *Not All Claps and Cheers: Humor in Business and Society Relationships*. Milton Park: Routledge.

For further reading on the effects of humor in groups and teams, see:

Fine, G. A., & De Soucey, M. (2005). Joking Cultures: Humor Themes as Social Regulation in Group Life. *Humor. International Journal of Humor Research*, *18*(1), 1–22.

Lyman, P. (1987). The fraternal bond as a joking relationship. A case study of the role of sexist jokes in male group bonding. In M. S. Kimmel (Ed.), *Changing men. New directions in research on men and masculinity*, pp. 143–153. Thousand Oaks, CA: Sage.

Romero, E.J. & Pescosolido, A. (2008). Humor and group effectiveness. *Human Relations, 61*(3), 395–418.

Terrion, J. L., & Ashforth, B. E. (2002). From 'I' to 'we': The role of putdown humor and identity in the development of a temporary group. *Human Relations, 55*(1), 55–87.

For comprehensive research on laughter, stress and other psychological and physiological aspects of humor, see:

Martin, R. A. (2007). *The psychology of humor. An integrative approach*. Burlington, MA., Elsevier.

For further reading about sex workers and humor, see:

Downe, P. J. (1999, January). Laughing when it hurts: Humor and violence in the lives of Costa Rican prostitutes. In *Women's Studies International Forum* (Vol. 22, No. 1, pp. 63–78). Pergamon.

The UK survey about time spent at work can be accessed at:

(http://www.news.com.au/finance/work/at-work/employees-average-two-hours-and-53-minutes-work-a-day-survey-shows/news-story/16e8136e776a db98faccd407433249a8)

Pollyanna is a 1913 novel by Eleanor H Parker. It is considered to be a children's literature classic. The name 'Pollyanna' has become a popular term for someone with a very optimistic (but perhaps naïve) outlook. (https://en.wikipedia.org/wiki/Pollyanna).

Monty Python's *Life of Brian*, is a 1979 British satirical, religious comedy film. It stars and was written by the comedy group Monty Python (Graham Chapman, John Cleese, Terry Gilliam, Eric Idle, Terry Jones and Michael Palin). (https://en.wikipedia.org/wiki/Monty_Python%27s_Life_of_Brian).

CHAPTER 9

100 best humor images can be found at:

(https://www.google.co.nz/search?source=hp&ei=zcm2WoUDi5fyBZb4psgM &q=100+best+humor+images&oq=100+best+humor+images&gs_l=psy-ab.3...2079.6427.0.7638.22.19.0.0.0.0.471.3227.2-9j2j1.12.0....0...1.1.64. psy-ab..10.11.3006.0..0j0i131k1j0i67k1j0i46i67k1j46i67k1j0i20i263k1j0i22 i30k1j33i22i29i30k1.0.whVKN5xf-Cc)

There are multiple sites with 'tips for workplace humor' such as:

(https://www.humorthatworks.com/how-to/10-tips-for-using-humor-in-the-workplace/)

(https://www.forbes.com/sites/mikemyatt/2012/04/12/8-tips-for-using-workplace-humor/#2577a4b67195)

(https://www.roberthalf.com/blog/salaries-and-skills/funny-stuff-5-tips-on-office-humor)

America's Funniest Home Videos can be seen at:

(http://afv.com/)

For further reading and strategies for dealing with offensive workplace humor, see:

Amy Gallo, (2018). 'How to respond to an offensive comment at work' *Harvard Business Review.* (https://hbr.org/2017/02/how-to-respond-to-an-offensive-comment-at-work)

The boxed description of the 'corporate bullshit generator' was adapted from:

The Corporate Bullshit Generator. (https://cbsg.sourceforge.io/cgi-bin/live).

The call center case we discuss comes from this workplace study:

Taylor, P., & Bain, P. (2003). 'Subterranean worksick blues': Humour as subversion in two call centres. *Organisation Studies, 24*(9), 1487–1509.

For further reading on the dark side of workplace humor, see:

Friedman, L.W. & Friedman, H.H. (2018). *Just kidding: when workplace humour is toxic.* In, Maon, François; Lindgreen, Adam; Vanhamme, Joelle; Angell, Robert; Memery, Juliet (eds). *Not All Claps and Cheers: Humor in Business and Society Relationships.* Milton Park: Routledge.

Plester, B. (2018). *Just a joke! A critical analysis of organizational humor.* In, Maon, François; Lindgreen, Adam; Vanhamme, Joelle; Angell, Robert; Memery, Juliet (eds). *Not All Claps and Cheers: Humor in Business and Society Relationships.* Milton Park: Routledge.

CHAPTER 10

We adapted some examples from 'The straight dope' message board for the plaintive blogger example. You can view this page at:

(https://boards.straightdope.com/sdmb/showthread.php?t=324478)

For further reading and strategies for dealing with offensive workplace humor, see:

Amy Gallo, (2018). 'How to respond to an offensive comment at work' *Harvard Business Review.* (https://hbr.org/2017/02/how-to-respond-to-an-offensive-comment-at-work)

Extra for experts: These are further high-quality studies that we have not cited in earlier chapters but that underpin our understanding of workplace humor.

For some extra reading on workplace humor and its effects, and for some interesting workplace studies, see:

Avolio, B. J., Howell, J. M., & Sosik, J. J. (1999). A funny thing happened on the way to the bottom line: Humor as a moderator of leadership style effects. *Academy of Management Journal, 42*(2), 219–227.

Bolton, S. C. & Houlihan, M. (2009). Are we having fun yet? A consideration of workplace fun and engagement. *Employee Relations, 31*(6), 556–568.

Bradney, P. (1957). The joking relationship in industry. *Human Relations, 10,* 179–187.

Collinson, D. (2002). Managing humour. *Journal of Management Studies, 39*(3), 269–289.

Cooper, C. (2005). Just joking around? *Employee humor expression as an ingratiatory behaviour. The Academy of Management Review, 30*(4), 765–776.

Coser, R. L. (1959). Some social functions of laughter. A study of humor in a hospital setting. *Human Relations, 12,* 171–181

Duncan, J. W., Smeltzer, L. R., & Leap, T. L. (1990). Humor and Work: Applications of joking behaviour to management. *Journal of Management, 16*(2), 255–279.

Fleming, P. (2005). Worker's playtime? Boundaries and cynicism in a 'Culture of fun' program. *The Journal of Applied Behavioral Science, 41*(3), 285–303.

Grugulis, I. (2002). Nothing Serious? Candidates' use of humour in management training. *Human Relations, 55*(4), 387–405.

Malone, P. B. (1980). Humor: A double-edged tool for today's managers? *Academy of Management Review, 5*(3), 357–361.

Morreall, J. (1983). *Taking laughter seriously*. Albany, NY: State University of New York.

Parker, M. (2007). The little book of management bollocks: Kitsch artefacts. In R. Westwood & C. Rhodes (Eds.), *Humour, work and organisation*, 77–91. London: Routledge.

Pelster, B. A. (2016) Complexity and chaos: Organizational humor and emotions. In Holly Phillips, *Humor: Emotional Aspects, Role in Social Interactions and Health Effects*.

Robert, C. & Yan, W. (2007). The case of developing new research on humour and culture in organizations: Toward a higher grade of manure. *Research in Personnel and Human Resources Management, 26*, 205–267

Romero, E. J., & Cruthirds, K. W. (2006). The use of humor in the workplace. *Academy of Management Perspectives, 20*(2), 58–70.

Tracy, S.J., Myers, K.K. & Scott, W. (2006). Cracking jokes and crafting selves: Sensemaking and identity management among human service workers. *Communication Monographs, 73*(3), 283–308.

Tyler, M. & Cohen, L. (2008). Management in/as comic relief: Queer theory and gender performativity in The Office. *Gender, Work and Organization, 15*(2), 114–132.

Warren, S., & Fineman, S. (2007). 'Don't get me wrong, it's fun here, but...' Ambivalence and paradox in a 'fun' work environment. In R. Westwood & C. Rhodes (Eds.), *Humour, work and organisation*, (pp. 92–112). London: Routledge.

Westwood, R. & Johnston, A. (2012). Reclaiming authentic selves: control, resistive humour and identity work in the office. *Organization, 19*(6), 787–808.

INDEX

© The Author(s) 2019   183
B. Plester, K. Inkson, *Laugh out Loud: A User's Guide to Workplace Humor*, https://doi.org/10.1007/978-981-13-0283-1